INVITATION TO GOETHE'S

FAUST

OTHER BOOKS BY
H.G. HAILE

Das Faustbuch nach der Wolenbüttler Handschrift

History of Doctor Johann Faustus Recovered from the
German

Artist in Chrysalis: A Biographical Study of Goethe
in Italy

Martin Luther and the Book: Forces Shaping Technology

INVITATION
TO GOETHE'S
FAUST

H.G. HAILE

Invitation to Goethe's Faust

Includes bibliographical references and index.

STUDIES IN THE HUMANITIES NO. 21

The University of Alabama Press

University, Alabama

Library of Congress Cataloging in Publication Data

Haile, Harry Gerald, 1931–
    Invitation to Goethe's Faust.

    Includes bibliographical references and index.
    1.   Goethe, Johann Wolfgang von, 1749–1832.   Faust.
I.   Title.
PT1925.H3   832'.6   77-7461
ISBN 0-8173-7326-8

CONTENTS

AUTHOR'S FOREWORD

At the time I wrote this book, I felt that certain important contentions about criticism were better advanced by deed than by argument. Now, as I read the proofs, I would also like to make two of my contentions explicit. Writing about literature is, I think, a very personal undertaking and should be frankly so. The corollary is that our subjective understanding of literature reveals our own unique time and place. The other, related assumption is that commentators on literature speak most productively to one another indirectly, when addressing themselves to their own contemporary countrymen.

As irony would have it, the late 1960s and early 1970s brought widespread crisis to university presses; publication of my "invitation" to Faust was delayed for some years. Even the 1975 revision could not be issued immediately. As a consequence, I am permitted now to face up to the question posed by those assumptions of mine: for just how long can such immediate, down-home criticism claim attention?

I am willing to let the reader judge. I have to admit that the early chapters now strike me as a bit plodding (but I don't know how else I would approach a general audience with an invitation to *Faust*), and the Epilogue may be a little sentimental; but as for the entire effort, I am even more eager than before to offer it as an example of traditional Humanism: an attempt to bring a distant classic to one's own people, in the confidence that this viewpoint is the ultimate test of literature.

I am grateful to The University of Alabama Press for bearing with me during these years and for publishing a book that often too openly snubs the guild. I also want to thank the University of Illinois Research Board for providing me generous research assistance, and Debbie Voigt for her faithful attention to the secondary literature in "Walpurgis Night Dream." If the myriad line references to *Faust* turn out to be accurate, then Linda DeMeritt gets the credit.

Summer, 1977

PREFACE

Literary criticism at the middle of the 20th century was preoccupied with methodological soundness by rigorous concentration on the text itself. The trammels of historicity on the one hand and of didacticism on the other had been cut away toward the end of the nineteenth century, as art began to be understood as something in need neither of extrinsic explanation nor of extrinsic justification, our own aesthetic response to it being conceived as a valuable experience. Such an orientation encouraged criticism in primarily structural terms and was quite in accord with contemporary art, which sprang from similar intellectual soil. Goethe's era, on the other hand, thought of literature in an entirely different way, as biographically conditioned expression directed toward some conscious purpose.

Ignoring for the moment theoretical questions of feasibility, I assume the fundamental need, if any, for writing about expressive literature must lie in facilitating communication between a poet and his modern audience, who are our own contemporaries and countrymen. The task is to seek out the poet's intention in order, where necessary, to make it readily intelligible in terms of current experience. It is clear that we cannot know whether the poet's intention is discoverable. We may steep ourselves in his personality and in his times to see if we can accommodate our minds to his radically different assumptions about nature, art, and society. We may try to be circumspect and diligent in spotting clues to his thinking and in tracking them down; still, we have to admit that we can achieve no more than an hypothesis, and probably a highly personalized one at that.

Once embarked on the uncertain sea of expressive literature from a distant place and time, we certainly do well to set our course by the relatively familiar outlines of our native shores. To which of the immense variety of problems in the *Faust* text should a critic address his efforts? Except for certain social assumptions which ask for just a little clarification, no one needs our prompting to appreciate the touching relationship between Gretchen and Faust. Faust's turn to magic, on the other hand, is a vital node in the poem which precisely our contemporaries have great difficulty taking seriously. If it can be discussed in terms of modern experience, then here might lie the sort of task to which we should give first priority.

We all know the truism that by reading great literature we can broaden our experience vicariously; it is a shallow kind of experience we come by in that way. In fact, the poet who is trying to communicate with us over the remove of centuries may in large measure be dependent on our own first-hand experience. A man of sheltered life and mild passions may remain untouched by a work which deeply affects another, who with Werther says: "I've been drunk more than once, and my passions were never far from madness." When we have loved, then we can apprehend and appreciate a poet's expression of loving; if we have ourselves long grappled with an intellectual problem, then we are already softened for the full impact of a poem which centers on it. We discover that we can re-read the same work at different times in our lives yet find it just as fresh at each reading, because we have brought to it on each occasion a new background in our own experience and hence an expanded personal receptivity. A fundamental task of the critic is to show how the human experiences on which the poet drew are analogous to those of the reader, especially when a remove of time or culture threatens to obscure that kinship.

I have organized my book around some of the major problems which make parts of *Faust* remote for the present age. After an Introduction which outlines the periods when Goethe worked on *Faust* as they recur throughout his productive career, my first effort goes toward bringing out the significance of this poem in his life— and in general the significance of poetry for a poet. Subsequent chapters (II–V) examine selected portions of *Faust* with a view toward characterizing that particular epoch in Goethe's intellectual and artistic development which produced each of them. Two middle chapters (VI and VII) are calculated to orient a modern mind with regard to "truth" and "fiction" around 1800. The Enlightenment had just succeeded in discrediting most of the trappings of Christianity, yet speculative philosophy was tending to reinforce faith in a transcendent reality. Our era has almost reversed that orientation. While more tolerant of institutionalized religion, we tend to dismiss, perhaps even impatiently, conjectures about immortality. Against this background I try to open up five fundamental problems of individual identity in *Faust* in as many chapters (VIII–XII).

Much more space goes to *Faust II* than to *Faust I*. This is not to suggest that *Faust II* is more important, just less accessible to Americans now. It is in the same sense that I turn relatively much effort to the preludes, the Walpurgis Nights, the Helen Act. Each chapter was written so as to be readable in itself, but my general contention that Faust is an exploration of individual consciousness assumes a consecutive reading. No more is attempted here than an invitation to poetry. Much, indeed most, of the delight of *Faust*, its delicate structure, complex themes, glorious language and imagery, and metric variety remain untouched here. I hope that my own remarks are above all readable, and that they always lead back to *Faust*.

I ask in all humility the forgiveness of my scholarly colleagues for what some may take to be impudence. Goethe and *Faust* have become monuments for German speakers, and German lands have laws (*Denkmalschutz*) to protect their monuments from modernization. Perhaps the only advantage enjoyed by a foreigner who did not grow up in the monument's shadow is that he stands somewhat freer of tradition and can hope to be indulged by those who are closer to it. That I am massively indebted to generations of *Faust* research will be obvious to scholars. Footnotes to acknowledge the debt in detail, or even to confess the various points where I may fall out of step with scholarly opinion, do not seem called for. I hope that my effort can be judged by layman and scholar alike in terms of its own aim, to avail 20th-century Americans of what I take to be a noble literary work of modern Europe.

INTRODUCTION

Goethe's work on *Faust* falls into four fairly distinct time spans. We know that

(1) some of *Faust* was written in the years 1773–1775, when the author was in his twenties;

(2) he tried to complete *Faust* in the late 1780's—his own late thirties—but had little success;

(3) he did make substantial progress just before the turn of the century;

(4) at last, the aged Goethe returned to *Faust* in the middle 1820's to work on it from time to time until his death, but more and more steadily as he approached, and passed, eighty.

1773–1775

Many have wandered into lengthy discussion as to when Goethe conceived *Faust* and when he first resolved to write such a work; we can be sure that he did actually set about it by the time of his last years at home in Frankfurt. The question why he failed to produce the completed work in the same years also entails elaborate explanation and conjecture. Let us observe only that what did take form certainly amounted to two quite discrete dramatic pieces.

One was a loosely connected group of monologues, dialogues, and skits which derive from the old Faust tradition as it survived out of the 16th century in chap books, in puppet plays, and in the popular mind of Germany:

> an opening monologue (lines 354–446),
> Faust's conjuration of spirits (447–521),
> a Faust-Wagner dialogue (522–605—but not 598–601),
> the Student-Mephistopheles dialogue (1868–2050),
> "Auerbach's Tavern" (2073–2336).

The other drama is not loose-knit at all, but one clear perception. The Gretchen plot seems to have possessed such immediacy for Goethe that he did not choose to develop it before us, but is able to disclose it in a series of ostensibly disconnected glimpses. Most of it was finished before 1775, i.e., the scenes from Faust's accosting Gretchen on the street, right on through the appearance of her brother and his first monologue (2605–3216 and 3374–3645); some of "Forest and Cavern" (3342–69); a snatch of Faust's return to Gretchen during her pregnancy (3650–69); "Cathedral" (3776–3834); and the revelation of Gretchen's fate in "Gloomy Day," as well as the final scenes of the tragedy (4399–4612).

This beautiful little stage play, entirely unrelated to the Faust tradition, derived from Goethe's own experience and fancy—but we must not forget that his extremely active imagination was at least as strongly stimulated by literary experience as by events, i.e., the Gretchen tragedy like most of the other works from Goethe's youth is bound up with literary models which he most admired. If we recognize close allusions to Ophelia in Gretchen, it might be because the entire episode was conceived in honest emulation of Shakespeare. Of course it is true that the fate of the unwed mother, a generally popular topic for speculation in the late 18th century, was especially much discussed by Goethe's circle as a consequence of the Frankfurt public execution of an unfortunate girl who had destroyed her unwanted infant. Goethe had been involved in love affairs himself, and he had probably fancied how an unusually serious one might take a tragic turn. It was always characteristic of him to imagine such *potential* experiences through—like Faust eager to savor "all that is the lot of human kind" in his own "senses' core" (1770). Although the execution occurred in January 1772, the Gretchen scenes may not have been written until a year or so later. "I know myself," Goethe once said, "and am aware that impressions made on me bear fruit at a much later time."

1788–1790

When he departed Weimar for Italy in 1786, Goethe had already begun preparing the first authorized edition of his works. *Faust* was one of the items which he hoped to include—and did, under the title: *Faust. Ein Fragment.* Either in Italy or shortly after his return he was able to complete three of those pieces for which he is most admired today: *Iphigenia, Egmont,* and *Tasso.* He could not finish *Faust,* but managed only a few short additions. The most important was "Witch's Kitchen." It connected the Faust skits with the Gretchen tragedy by trying to make plausible that drastic change in age and temperament from the mature scholar of the early scenes to the hot young lover who claims he can seduce Gretchen in a matter of hours. Like the other short additions (1770–1867 and 3217–3341), "Witch's Kitchen" is characterized by a heightened sense of compositional technique and a remarkable freedom of association. Whether written in Italy or shortly after his return, they could be used to characterize his development there.

1797–1806

Like the earlier subtitle, "A Fragment," the very designation "Part I" conceded that the work as published in 1806 was still incomplete. Nevertheless, the effort at the end of the century does represent Goethe's first really protracted work on *Faust,* when he applied to it the will and resolve which was in fact a first vouchsafe of its importance to him and a promise of its completion if he but lived long enough.

On 24 June, 1797—a date which Goethe in later years celebrated as *Faust's* birthday—he wrote "Dedication." "Prologue in Heaven" as well as an extensive plan for the entire drama date from this same summer. During subsequent years he not only worked forward (e.g., "Outside the City Gates" and "Study Room"), he turned to other parts of a now extensive plan, added "Walpurgis Night" to the Gretchen drama, complemented "Prologue in Heaven" by writing a part of Act V, and he indited a few hundred lines of the Helen episode which we still have in the form he gave them in 1800.

Mephistopheles posed a problem. The early sketches had left off at Wagner's exit and taken up again when Mephistopheles in professor's robes advises a freshman. Nothing existed as yet to explain his presence—unless we take the Earth Spirit's parting shot not merely as scorn of Faust, but also as an allusion to Mephisto:

512   Du gleichst dem Geist, den du begreifst,
      Nicht mir!

      Thou'rt like the Spirit which thou comprehendest,
      Not me!

Actually Mephistopheles represented only one chore among many
in the larger task of filling out what Goethe came to call *die grosse
Lücke*—"the big gap": lines 606–1867. In April 1801, he even referred to the group of scenes in which Faust and Mephistopheles
make their agreement (and on which the whole poem theoretically
hinges) as "a work in its own right." Had *Faust* been completed in
these years, it might have been a much more uniform work.

1825–1831

Another generation passed before he gave serious thought to the
poem again. When he turned back to the Helen Act in early 1825, it
may have been as a way of coming to terms with changing times, for
he published it now under the title "Helen. Classic-Romantic Phan-
tasmagory" (he completed it on *Faust*'s "birthday," 1826). Throughout 1827 and 1828, his diary is marked by regular records of what he
called *das Hauptgeschäft* and *das Hauptwerk*—"the main job." Efforts in Acts I, II, and V progressed side by side, leaving most of Act
IV to be filled in later. The old man approaching eighty commented:

> I am able to work now on the second part of my *Faust* only in the
> early hours, when I feel refreshed and strengthened by sleep and am
> not yet distraught by the foolish spectres of the day. But what comes
> of it? With the very best of luck one page of manuscript. Usually,
> however, only enough to cover what you can span with your hand.
> Often, when my condition is less productive, even less.

On 21 July 1831 he recorded: *Abschluß des Hauptgeschäfts*—
"conclusion of the main job."

The very next day he entered: *Das Hauptgeschäft zustande
gebracht*—"the main job completed." In fact, he spent four more
weeks on Act IV, but then he wrote: "From now on I can look upon
my life as a pure gift, and it does not make a bit of difference any

more whether—or what I do." He sealed *Faust* in an envelope and refused to discuss it until it might appear in his collected works. On 9 January 1832, however, he opened the envelope and read from the work to his daughter-in-law. On 24 January he recorded: "New *Faust* urge as regards better execution of the main motifs which, in finishing, I treated all too laconically." Goethe died on 22 March.

In conclusion to the exceptionally complex history of the composition of *Faust*, let us refer briefly to the important events in its publication record. Although unauthorized editions of Goethe's collected works had occurred as early as 1775, he made no effort to publish anything more than individual pieces before the time of his Italian trip, when he prepared for Göschen in Leipzig: *Goethe's Schriften*, 8 vols. 1787–1790. Volume VII gave *Faust* to the public for the first time, as *Ein Fragment*. It begins with the famous monologue (354 ff.) and continues through Wagner's exit (605), takes up again with the present line 1770 and continues through the Student scene, "Auerbach's Tavern," "Witch's Kitchen," and thus into the Gretchen drama. For reasons which we can only guess, Goethe cut the tragedy off abruptly at the end of "Cathedral," where Gretchen calls out:

3834   Nachbarin! Euer Fläschchen!

Neighbor! Your smelling-bottle!

The first comprehensive edition of Goethe's works by his permanent publisher, Cotta in Tübingen, brought the entire *Faust I* in Volume VIII (1808): *Faust. Der Tragödie erster Theil—Faust. The First Part of the Tragedy.*

The last edition of his works during his lifetime was the famous *Vollständige Ausgabe letzter Hand* in forty volumes. Volume IV (1827) contained the text which later became Act III, but here it was entitled: *Helena. Klassisch-Romantische Phantasmagorie. Zwischenspiel zu Faust*—"Interlude to *Faust*." Volume XII (1828) reprinted *Faust I* and went on as far as line 6036 of *Faust II*. At the bottom of the page stands the remark: *Ist fortzusetzen*—"to be continued." Nothing more of *Faust* appeared while Goethe lived. His last surviving letter is to Wilhelm von Humboldt, who had expressed interest in the rest of *Faust II.* Goethe responds:

> It would without question give me infinite pleasure to dedicate and confide these very serious jests to my dear, gratefully acknowledged, far-flung friends while I am still alive. But the times are truly so ridiculous and muddled that I am convinced my honest efforts, so long prosecuted in behalf of this rare structure, would be ill rewarded and driven aground like a derelict to lie there in ruins for the time being, buried in the sands of the moment. Confusing theories guiding confusing actions rule over the world.

Twenty additional volumes entitled *Goethes nachgelassene Werke* were added to the forty of the *Ausgabe letzter Hand* after his death. The first—out already in 1832—contained *Faust. Der Tragödie zweiter Theil in fünf Akten—Faust. The Second Part of the Tragedy in Five Acts.*

In 1887, the scholar Erich Schmidt recognized in the Weimar archives a *Faust* manuscript in the hand of Louise von Göchhausen, a lady-in-waiting on the Dowager Duchess of Goethe's day. Apparently prior to the earliest publication of *Faust*, it lacks some of the scenes of *Faust. Ein Fragment*, e.g., "Witch's Kitchen" and most of "Forest and Cavern." Some scenes are in prose instead of verse: Mephistopheles' advice to the Student, "Auerbach's Tavern," and "Dungeon." The most exciting aspect of Erich Schmidt's discovery was that the manuscript contains the end of the Gretchen tragedy. Here was proof that those impressive final scenes had indeed been part of the early conception.

Erich Schmidt entitled his discovery somewhat pompously: *Faust in ursprünglicher Gestalt—Faust in its original form.* He also called it the *Urfaust*, and this is the way some scholars refer to it still. Inasmuch as the manuscript is a copy made probably without Goethe's knowledge or permission, it would be going too far to assume that he regarded the material which lay before the Lady Göchhausen as anything more than preparatory sketches, whereas the title which has become attached to her manuscript implies that it is one of his works.

For Sweet Nellie Clyde

INVITATION TO GOETHE'S

FAUST

Faust is quoted from the Artemis Gedenk-Ausgabe.
English metrical quotations are from the Bayard Taylor translation.
Nonmetrical English renderings are mine.

—H. G. HAILE

I

THE POEM'S MEANING FOR THE POET

DEDICATION

Here is the first challenge. It is concentrated poetry in which each line means a great deal. The reader must participate by exerting relatively much effort while reading. He must proceed with eyes wide open and his fancy active.

I, timorous teacher, am always concerned that my students are going to miss something, and of course they do. These lines are written from the fullness of a half-century's experience. Not only did Goethe have almost fifty years to look back on; during those years he had done a great deal of looking back. My young students are not intimately acquainted with his life, can only guess at the content of his reminiscences; but this is not so important as the fact that they themselves have not yet accumulated much experience of their own to reflect about and may not be able to appreciate retrospection itself. The poet is asking not only that his reader be ready with imaginative response to his poem; he hopes also that he will know something of life, because common human experience is ultimately the fundamental medium of communication between poet and reader.

The title might more precisely have been translated "Appropriation," or "Adoption." It is customary, all right, to begin a longer work with a "Dedication," and that is one possible way of understanding German *Zueignung*. What we read about here, however, is a poet's *owning* of his work and the past which attaches to it. We must seek to read in sympathetic understanding for a man of forty-eight who now at last dedicates himself to a project which he has repeatedly spurned during his mature years: some drama fragments written by a youth in his twenties, together with the poignant associations which they evoke.

By no means did Goethe work continuously on *Faust* during all the years that came to stretch between original conception and final touches, but it did all that time lodge in his mind, intermittently to be called to the fore, sometimes in distaste, sometimes as the object of intense work. To say that it became closely intertwined in the history of his personality as he grew older could be only an understatement, but *Faust* is by no means unique in this respect. Two generalizations can be made about virtually all Goethe's more successful works: They originated as intense personal expression; they took final form only long after inception, in some cases resting in the depth of his mind to be mulled over, reshaped, forgotten and recollected again over a space of years (*Götz von Berlichingen, Egmont, Iphigenia, Tasso, The Sorrows of Young Werther*), or even decades (*Wilhelm Meister, Faust*). For Goethe the creative process was closely related to constant preoccupation with the history of his own personality.

In our day clarity of understanding about one's past is considered to have important therapeutic value. One of Goethe's most famous descriptions of a successful depth analysis occurs when Iphigenia forces her deranged brother Orestes to open channels of memory leading back into their childhood. It is a moment in which the man confronts himself in terms of his past. He weeps—weeps as does Goethe here when his conscious mind opens to healthful awareness of what he once was years ago. Weeping amounts in both instances to a dissolving of the shells which have encrusted our personality. Tears flow at the moment when a heretofore constricted conscious is relieved and quickened by open reaches in time, the dimension of the psyche's history and true existence.

Since questions about the history of individual personality are pertinent to Goethe's creative drive, I shall be returning to them occasionally. *Faust* was itself a great factor in Goethe's own development—and thus we may come upon the best way of stating the theme of "Dedication." A fifty-year-old turns his mind again to forgotten surroundings and early friends as they were perceived by the less lucid (*trüb*) eye of a twenty-year-old; mature objectivity recalls the creatures of a young man's fancy. The topic of "Dedication" is the importance of one of these creatures for the history of Goethe's own development: *Faust*.

PRELUDE IN THE THEATER

This middle prelude holds the two others together like links in a chain. While irony and good humor most effectively interrelate the second two, the important common theme shared by "Dedication" and "Prelude in the Theater" is more serious: the poet's bond with his poetry. The expansive Manager, while cooly aware of what audiences are like and accustomed to calculating their response, feels quite dependent on the public, hence anxious (43 ff.), but the Comic Character has a sure sense of what will go over:

86   Laßt Phantasie mit allen ihren Chören,
       Vernunft, Verstand, Empfindung, Leidenschaft,
       Doch, merkt Euch wohl! nicht ohne Narrheit hören!

       Let Fancy be with her attendants fitted,
       Sense, Reason, Sentiment, and Passion join,
       But have a care, lest Folly be omitted!

His sympathies do lie primarily with the Poet, but like the Manager he appreciates the profitable implications of creativity as well. In the irony that results we may feel we hear Goethe speaking most directly, e.g., concerning the audience:

179   Ein jeder sieht, was er im Herzen trägt.
       Noch sind sie gleich bereit, zu weinen und zu lachen,
       Sie ehren noch den Schwung, erfreuen sich am Schein;
       Wer fertig ist, dem ist nichts recht zu machen,
       Ein Werdender wird immer dankbar sein.

       For each beholds what in his bosom lurks.
       They still are moved at once to weeping or to laughter,
       Still wonder at your flights, enjoy the show they see:

> A mind, once formed, is never suited after;
> One yet in growth will ever grateful be.

His attachment to the ones "in growth" is what really lends the
Comic Character understanding for the sentiments already expressed in "Dedication." He, too, is aware of the tremendous importance of the time dimension for personality. In "Dedication" the
poet Goethe surveyed the labyrinthine path which wandered from
his youthful conception to his maturer efforts with it. Now the
Comic Character urges such *alte Herrn*—"aged sirs"—to take courage, to continue the "sweet digression"—*holdes Irren*—it being
only at their time of life that a true overview of the past all the way
back to childhood becomes possible.

206   Doch ins bekannte Saitenspiel
        Mit Mut und Anmut einzugreifen,
        Nach einem selbstgesteckten Ziel
        Mit holdem Irren hinzuschweifen,
        Das, alte Herrn, ist eure Pflicht,
        Und wir verehren euch darum nicht minder.
        Das Alter macht nicht kindisch, wie man spricht,
        Es findet uns nur noch als wahre Kinder.

        But that familiar harp with soul
        To play,—with grace and bold expression,
        And towards a self-erected goal
        To walk with many a sweet digression,
        This, aged Sirs, belongs to you,
        And we no less revere you for that reason:
        Age childish makes, they say, but 't is not true;
        We're only genuine children still, in Age's season!

Recollection of the irretrievable past, the poignancy of early
memories for the now mature man, the importance of his personal
history in the creative process and the halting question whether age
and creativity are not mutually exclusive—in alluding to such ap-
prehensions the Comic Character sharpens our awareness of a poet's
relationship to poetry.

"Dedication" lamented the passing of those who were once sympathetic with Goethe's work (his *Lied* or *Leid*, depending on the reading one may prefer).

17   Sie hören nicht die folgenden Gesänge,
       Die Seelen, denen ich die ersten sang;
       Zerstoben ist das freundliche Gedränge,
       Verklungen, ach! der erste Widerklang.
       Mein Lied ertönt der unbekannten Menge,
       Ihr Beifall selbst macht meinem Herzen bang.

       They hear no longer these succeeding measures,
       The souls, to whom my earliest songs I sang:
       Dispersed the friendly troop, with all its pleasures,
       And still, alas! the echoes first that rang!
       I bring the unknown crowd my treasures;
       Their very plaudits give my heart a pang.

Anxious about the "unknown crowd," Goethe does not want to please it. Precisely on this subject the robust voice of the Manager opens "Prologue in the Theater":

37   Ich wünschte sehr, der Menge zu behagen.

       I wish the crowd to feel itself well treated.

He dwells on it:

49   Denn freilich mag ich gern die Menge sehen,
       Wenn sich der Strom nach unsrer Bude drängt.

       For 't is my pleasure to behold the crowd
       When to our booth the current sets apace,

Thus the first words from the Poet pertain to the crowd, too:

59   O sprich mir nicht von jener bunten Menge.

       Speak not to me of yonder motley crowd

He finds it cold, forbidding and impersonal. Childlike, he longs for warmth, friendliness, coziness in a quiet—as he puts it—*Himmelsenge:*

63   Nein, führe mich zur stillen Himmelsenge,
      Wo nur dem Dichter reine Freude blüht,
      Wo Lieb und Freundschaft unsres Herzens Segen
      Mit Götterhand erschaffen und erpflegen!

      No, lead me to a quiet heavenly niche
      Where alone for the poet pure joy blooms
      Where love and friendship with divine hand
      Create and nurture our heart's blessing.

This, of course, is the idea expressed in "Dedication" (compare line 65 with line 12): genuine happiness has both its origin and continuance in love and kindness. In "Dedication" Goethe connected this perception with lost friendships of the remote past. The Poet, too, speaks of the past:

67   Ach! was in tiefer Brust uns da entsprungen,
      Was sich die Lippe schüchtern vorgelallt

      Ah, what arose then deep in our hearts,
      What tender lips timidly murmured

Their emotional bond with the past accounts for the closest relationship between the Poet and Goethe of "Dedication." Both are emotionally attached to their poetic creation because of its great significance in the history of creative personality:

11   Gleich einer alten, halbverklungnen Sage
      Kommt erste Lieb und Freundschaft mit herauf;
      Der Schmerz wird neu, es wiederholt die Klage
      Des Lebens labyrinthisch irren Lauf.

      And, like an old and half-extinct tradition,
      First Love returns, with Friendship in his train.
      Renewed is Pain: with mournful repetition
      Life tracks his devious, labyrinthine chain.

It is as if the creative individual—or the creative stratum of personality—attached primary importance to its own developmental path. As a consequence, that particular time of life characterized by development, with the acute selfconsciousness and subjectivity which attends changing personality, is especially treasured:

184   DICHTER.   So gib mir auch die Zeiten wieder,
       Da ich noch selbst im Werden war,
       Da sich ein Quell gedrängter Lieder
       Ununterbrochen neu gebar,
       Da Nebel mir die Welt verhüllten,
       Die Knospe Wunder noch versprach,
       Da ich die tausend Blumen brach,
       Die alle Täler reichlich füllten!
       Ich hatte nichts und doch genug:
       Den Drang nach Wahrheit und die Lust am Trug!
       Gib ungebändigt jene Triebe,
       Das tiefe, schmerzenvolle Glück,
       Des Hasses Kraft, die Macht der Liebe,
       Gib meine Jugend mir zurück!

       POET.   Then give me back that time of pleasures,
       While yet in joyous growth I sang,
       When, like a fount, the crowding measures
       Uninterrupted gushed and sprang!
       Then bright mist veiled the world before me,
       In opening buds a marvel woke,
       As I the thousand blossoms broke,
       Which every valley richly bore me!
       I nothing had, and yet enough for youth
       Joy in Illusion, ardent thirst for Truth.
       Give, unrestrained, the old emotion,
       The bliss that touched the verge of pain,
       The strength of Hate, Love's deep devotion,
       O, give me back my youth again!

This is not praise of youth merely for youth's sake. The Poet recognizes that in the last analysis it is the element of time which is really fundamental to his work:

67   Ach! was in tiefer Brust uns da entsprungen,
      Was sich die Lippe schüchtern vorgelallt,
      Mißraten jetzt und jetzt vielleicht gelungen,
      Verschlingt des wilden Augenblicks Gewalt.
      Oft, wenn es erst durch Jahre durchgedrungen,
      Erscheint es in vollendeter Gestalt.

      Ah, what arose then deep in our hearts,
      What tender lips timidly murmured
      Now jumbled, now perhaps well phrased
      Was lost in the wild rush of the moment
      Often, only after surviving for years
      Does it take on a perfect form.

It is not essential that a poet *be* young, only that he have been
young. It may even await the older man best to lend expressive form
to that "wild rush of the moment" experienced in his youthful past.

If the last quoted lines (71–72) survey a stretch of time from age
back to youth, the Poet is also concerned about time's extension
forward:

71   Oft, wenn es erst durch Jahre durchgedrungen,
      Erscheint es in vollendeter Gestalt.
      Was glänzt, ist für den Augenblick geboren;
      Das Echte bleibt der Nachwelt unverloren.

      Often, only after surviving for years
      Does it take on a perfect form.
      What glitters is made for the moment
      What's genuine is not lost to posterity.

He writes *about* past experience and not about the present instant;
he writes *for* future generations, not for the fleeting moment. The
Poet would assure channels of communication forward in time for
men yet unborn; his power to do so flows out of his own developmental history.

If the personality can open to the flow of time, can it not open in
other respects, too? The fifty-year-old is quite a different man from
his twenty-year-old self. If the one personality can nevertheless
attain sympathetic understanding for the other, cannot similar

mutual understandings be achieved in the present instant? We are no longer confined within our specific individuality, our hearts can beat in unison with the rest of creation. The Poet calls this *das Menschenrecht* (136)—"the right of man," "his highest right" (135):

142   Wenn die Natur des Fadens ew'ge Länge,
    Gleichgültig drehend, auf die Spindel zwingt,
    Wenn aller Wesen unharmon'sche Menge
    Verdrießlich durcheinanderklingt:
    Wer teilt die fließend immer gleiche Reihe
    Belebend ab, daß sie sich rhythmisch regt?
    Wer ruft das Einzelne zur allgemeinen Weihe,
    Wo es in herrlichen Akkorden schlägt?

    When on the spindle, spun to endless distance,
    By Nature's listless hand the thread is twirled,
    And the discordant tones of all existence
    In sullen jangle are together hurled,
    Who, then, the changeless orders of creation
    Divides, and kindles into rhythmic dance?
    Who brings the One to join the general ordination,
    Where it may throb in grandest consonance?

Should it not be called the highest privilege, *das Menschenrecht*, to impart meaning to creation? Harmony cannot be determined objectively in the world: it is in the appreciative eye of the beholder. The integrity of the universe, if any, is dependent on the sympathetic understanding of an individual. Unlike other creatures, man knowingly thrills to Nature, his interpretive response deriving beauty from an otherwise indifferent clatter. We can discover elsewhere in works from Goethe's middle years this same idea that man is the final, essential ingredient of the universe because he alone endows Nature with meaning. It is in this way that man enables man to believe in God—the message of one of his most famous poems, *Das Göttliche*.

The view of man as the crowning touch of creation is not by any means new with Goethe. We are all familiar with the Sermon on the Mount: "Ye are the salt of the earth." In Jesus' view it amounts to an obligation on man: "So let your light shine before men that they may

see your good works and glorify your Father which is in heaven."
Das Göttliche draws a very similar corollary, but in the Poet's view
it is he, the Poet himself, and not man in general who answers for
man's responsibility to vindicate God in sympathetic perception of
His Creation:

156   Wer sichert den Olymp? vereinet Götter?
       Des Menschen Kraft, im Dichter offenbart!

       Who makes Olympus sure, the Gods uniting?
       The might of Man, as in the Bard revealed.

The poet becomes man *par excellence.* He differs from other men on
account of his personality or, more precisely, on account of his
immediate access to his own personal development out of the past.
Here is the important bond between the first two preludes to *Faust:*
both deal with the personality of the poet, both stress the dimension
of time and the poet's special need to expand in that continuum.

Rather than proceed therefore through *Faust* as we have it before
us in the final version, I am going to turn first to that part which
Goethe wrote when he was youngest, to see if a glimpse of its
earliest meaning for the poet is possible. Holding then to chronolog-
ical sequence during the first few chapters may help bring out the
stratification of the work, and in part account for the impression of
tremendous depth which it leaves upon the reader.

II

EARLY
COMPOSITION

Since the Göchhausen Manuscript probably comprises almost all Goethe's early work with *Faust*, it is especially useful as evidence of what those beginnings were. Fragmented though the old collation may at first glance appear, all the scenes in it do have a common denominator—they pertain in one way or another to academic life as the young Goethe experienced it: a serious search for and questioning of knowledge; an emotionally exhausting involvement with a girl.

The academy itself is presented in four scenes or skits. On the one hand there is Faust, who has exhausted fashionable channels of learning and is honest enough to admit it. Just to make sure that we understand what is *not* to be recognized as true knowledge, Wagner steps forward: one with naive faith in the learning process. A third aspect of academic life is the poor freshman encountering his adviser for the first time. Finally, no presentation of the university would be complete without the more advanced students in their natural habitat, the beer cellar. The professor who recognizes the futility of the academic process is made to appear admirable; he dares to seek new modes of knowing. The assistant with uncritical faith in academic endeavor is made to appear contemptible; he is hopelessly lost in a desert of parchment, ink, and dry facts. The typical student, who believes his professor, is seen as a dupe; his adviser, a cynical devil. We have here a point of view which has been shared by countless serious students at many times and places, thus it is natural for us to suppose that the conception of the material may date back to Goethe's own student days.

Only the poet with his powerful fancy can "feel down to his

senses' core" (1771) the lot both of professor and student—or is there another who can? The magus Faust could have been transformed, with the aid of his spirits, from a mature professor into a bold young rake of twenty. Here may lie one of Goethe's reasons for choosing that sorcerer as title hero, because the other, all-important experience of student life is an affair with a town girl.

This particular sort of involvement may have ceased to be so well understood in the United States some time after World War II, as we began to achieve our ideal of higher education for all classes *and* both sexes. In Goethe's time attendance at the university was what it long continued to be even in this country: one of several rather obvious marks of belonging to a social elite—for young gentlemen only. Faust of the Gretchen tragedy is an educated man, hence probably a member of the middle class, i.e., that moneyed, educated city merchant and professional folk whom the Germans call "patrician." Gretchen is probably of the artisan and innkeeper class. Her father

3117   . . . hinterließ ein hübsch Vermögen
          Ein Häuschen und ein Gärtchen vor der Stadt.

          . . . left a nice estate,
          A house, a little garden near the town.

but there remains a tremendous social distance between her and the independently wealthy. Her background, language, and manners testify to a social difference which never allows the question of marriage with Faust to arise. All this is taken for granted at the very outset. He tries to pick her up with an approach which could not occur to him if she were of his own set. Hence his actions give his words the lie:

2605   Mein schönes Fräulein! Darf ich wagen,
       Meinen Arm und Geleit Ihr anzutragen?

       Fair lady, let it not offend you,
       That arm and escort I would lend you!

Her forthright answer

607   Bin weder Fräulein, weder schön

I'm neither lady, neither fair

sets things straight right away: "It is clear to both of us what is on *your* mind. I'll have nothing to do with you, Sir."

While the Gretchen tragedy is treated with great sympathy, the earlier scenes in the Göchhausen Manuscript tend toward satire: a sardonic view of the university faculty, a cynical exposure of the townspeople who gouge the students, and a travesty of students and citizens carousing in a beer hall. Few traditional figures can have appeared better suited to purposes of parody and burlesque than that ridiculous puppet-play character, Doctor Faustus, whose bombast was couched in ancient, crude *Knittelvers* (the four-beat line with an indeterminate number of unaccented syllables which Goethe imitates in some of these early scenes). The student scene was so outspokenly ribald that it had to suffer radical revision before Goethe felt he could include it in his first publication of *Faust*. To seek out the young author in his twenties on the grounds of his own most burning interests, we can best turn to the first 250 lines of "Night." University students undergoing analogous experiences, beset by similar frustrations and aspirations, surely have the very best possibility of reading "Night" sympathetically; but we were all twenty at some time or other, and everyone can enjoy these beginnings of *Faust* for himself, without the hindrance of detailed comment. I shall limit myself to some very general remarks which seem fundamental.

LINES 354–605

Although the early 16th century—when the historical Faust lived—long fascinated Goethe as especially characteristic in German history, he shows remarkably little antiquarian curiosity about his subject—only one of the traditional adventures, for example, is significantly reflected in the Göchhausen Manuscript ("Auerbach's Tavern"). The mere fact that Faust is a figure out of the German past was enough to carry the clear implication to Goethe's contemporaries: "Your drives and frustrations are not peculiar to your lives, but are part of the lot of man. You see with what immediacy, how convincingly they arise even in the breast of this absurd puppet Doctor Faustus, denizen of those ancient, dark and troubled times which had so little in common with your modern, enlightened and urbane Europe." Implicit in Goethe's choice of topic out of a bygone era is the argument that his themes are timeless. If the events—in so far as their fundamental import for mankind is concerned—might just as well have transpired in the 16th as in the 18th century, then they might also be projected onto the superficial 20th-century fabric. This is not to say that Goethe succeeded in producing a work which is timeless. It does seem fairly clear, however, that he tried.

From the epoch of the historical Doctor Faustus he drew two important themes: Occultism and Humanism. Each is often regarded as a peculiarly 15th- or 16th-century German trend. Both indeed flourished around 1500, and both have seemed to be outstanding contributions of Germany to Western Civilization. Goethe allowed each to become a dominant chord in "Night." A brief excursus on each may offer useful background for a modern reader.

With his very first words (522 ff.) Wagner seeks to identify himself with the Humanists, those men who in the 1400's and 1500's undertook to transfer the classical literary heritage to modern Europe. They were scholars of the Northern Renaissance and mostly associated with the burgeoning new universities of their day. Although they may in a large sense have been carrying forward the tradition of the medieval *trivium*, they laid much greater emphasis on profane texts and especially on the linguistic skills needed to appreciate the *Quellen* (562 f.). Men like Erasmus of Rotterdam were apparently convinced that these classical sources represented a nobler civilization than theirs, so that they conceived their own role as bridging the "dark" ages which separated themselves and their countrymen from the Ancients.

Some of the Humanists—the best known perhaps Philipp Melanchthon (1497–1560)—came to exert tremendous influence on the course of Western education at both university and pre-university levels, and eventually in Catholic as well as in Protestant lands. As a consequence of their attitudes schooling came more and more to be characterized by study of the classics both in Latin and Greek. Humanism conceived of primarily educational goals and of linguistic means for achieving them. The implications for the history of education were far reaching, as language and literature studies provided the core curriculum both of university and secondary education during a period in Europe extending from the 16th into the 20th century.

In Wagner, so strongly interested in what he calls *der Vortrag*—"delivery"—(524 ff., 546) and in the literary text (560 ff.), we recognize the mainstream of education in the Western World:

1104   Wie anders tragen uns die Geistesfreuden
       Von Buch zu Buch, von Blatt zu Blatt!
       Da werden Winternächte hold und schön,
       Ein selig Leben wärmet alle Glieder,
       Und ach, entrollst du gar ein würdig Pergamen,
       So steigt der ganze Himmel zu dir nieder!

       How otherwise the mental raptures bear us
       From page to page, from book to book!
       Then winter nights take liveliness untold,
       As warmer life in every limb had crowned you;
       And when your hands unroll some parchment rare and old,
       All Heaven descends, and opens bright around you!

Scholars have been unwilling to accept him as a representative of Humanism, much less as a typical educator. Some have preferred to adopt a narrower view which lets him represent the 18th-century Enlightenment: thus Wagner embodies trends peculiar to Goethe's own day, not ours, and we are tempted to read *Faust* observing

573   wie wirs zuletzt so herrlich weit gebracht.

    what grand progress we have made.

Goethe chose a Humanist in whom to satirize pedants of the 18th century—but certainly also pedants of Faust's 16th, and of our 20th century as well. We should see reflected in Wagner not just some fusty old Humanist, nor some dry-as-dust Rationalist, but above all the confident academic of the 1970's, sure of his procedures and criteria, of his sociology or economic theory. Wagner is an eternal type in the academic world: the gullible researcher so confident his research is worth while that it never occurs to him to relate a narrow field of study to the larger concerns and characteristic hopes of mankind. Faust shakes his head and wonders

602   Wie nur dem Kopf nicht alle Hoffnung schwindet,
       Der immerfort an schalem Zeuge klebt,
       Mit gier'ger Hand nach Schätzen gräbt,
       Und froh ist, wenn er Regenwürmer findet!

       How hope does not abandon such a brain
       That clings forever to such shallow stuff!
       Which digs with eager hand for buried ore,
       And, when it finds an angle-worm, rejoices!

Yet is not Faust a member of academia, too? What does he have against angle-worm research? Probably nothing, so long as the worms are not valued in themselves without thought to the only really interesting questions about them: what relationship do "angle-worms" bear to me, to the rest of Nature, and to God. Such inquiry would lead Wagner into Occultism, the sphere of Faust's current endeavor. It is the other important theme which Goethe drew from the 16th century.

Certain pagan religions adore Nature as herself a deity; others, as the primordial matrix whence arose both gods and men. Christian thought has also assumed an integral universe in the sense that it manifests one Creation and a Creator who knows when each sparrow falls. The elaborate systems of an Alfred North Whitehead or of an Albert Einstein are recent secular interpretations of our universe which also seek to interrelate all its depths by means of "general theories," be they logical or mathematical. When Goethe, himself a pioneer in the field of comparative anatomy, succeeded in confirming man's osteological kinship with the other mammalia, he too illustrated man's age-old drive to perceive Nature as one entity. The touching assumption popular among physicists and biologists of our time that intelligent life must have emerged elsewhere in the universe is a kind of final corollary to the assurance obtained by 19th-century spectroscopy that the heavens contain elements familiar here on earth. Nuclear physics, which permits us to understand elements as consisting of the same fundamental particles, and quantum mechanics, which has even subjected matter and radiation to one set of principles, offer our time its ultimate vindication of Nature and of the ways of God to man. The quest for such insight by spiritual and alchemical means a few centuries ago was called Occultism.

The sign of the macrocosm by which Faust seeks illumination (430 ff.) is an Occult symbol of confidence in the perfect relationship between the tiny world of man and Creation at large. His somewhat more successful but at last equally futile contemplation of the sign of the Earth Spirit should probably be taken in the same context. On the one hand Faust finds the traditional concepts of Occultism empty (*ein Schauspiel nur*, 454), but then he must also admit that his own faculties would not be equal to his goal in any case (517).

Nevertheless, Faust's turn to Occultism is certainly a serious effort to comprehend the universe, and we can no more dismiss it as a quaint relic of bygone days than we can take Wagner's Humanism as something foreign to us. To regard the hopes which Faust places in magic as possible only in earlier, stupider times is to be naive about the poem itself and blandly uncritical of current endeavor. Magic does, of course, make the assumption that ununderstood forces invest nature.

382   Das ich erkenne, was die Welt
       Im Innersten zusammenhält,
       Schau alle Wirkenskraft und Samen.

       That I may detect the inmost force
       Which binds the world, and guides its course;
       Its germs, productive powers explore.

The assumption of unknown causes, however, is not limited to magic: it is the starting point of all basic research. True science is not an inventory of the sure facts, but a grappling with the unknown. We have to assume that Faust's years as a student of theology were already directed toward finding "the inmost force / which binds the world and guides its course," but theology failed him. Other fields of research have failed him, too. At the outset of the poem we find him turning to Occultism, testing magic.

The serious reader is going to have to give some thought to how he himself would define "magic." The poem begins with Faust's earnest espousal of it. At last, as an old man, he deprecates its use and longs to confront Nature *ein Mann allein* (11404 ff.)—directly and unencumbered. If we are content to think of "magic" as a resort to the "supernatural," we shall be making an assumption that some kind of dichotomy exists in our universe: on the one hand the natural world, on the other the "supernatural." Neither Goethe nor our own time can accept that assumption. Do we really want to talk about "magic" as something which neither poet nor reader believes in? Perhaps so: that would be to renounce common grounds with Faust, practitioner of magic. Our own success, if such it be, in explaining magic out of our lives and recognizing magic as something only primitives believe in may then cut us off from a long poem that begins and ends in quite serious reference to *magic* as something of great importance in a man's relationship to Nature. If it is so important, can we not come to terms acceptable both to ourselves and to Faust?

There certainly is a clear dichotomy in the world as we and he perceive it: some phenomena can be accounted for to our satisfaction; others cannot. Since it is among these ununderstood phenomena that the "supernatural" is commonly sought, we might define *magic* as *the attempt to accomplish specific ends by means not fully understood.* This definition has the merit of satisfying the practitioner of magic and the enlightened skeptic alike. It does include, however, some everyday modern activities. For many of us, merely turning on an electric light is accomplishment of an end by means understood only to those sorcerers, the electrical engineers.

How is it with the electrical engineer? Is electricity magic, by our definition, to him? He knows how to use it as a means to accomplish *many* specific ends: is his overview of electronic potentials the same as understanding? Suppose Faust should insist that by *understanding* he means to *confront* directly and unhindered (11406)? Suppose he insists that he means experience, first-hand knowledge? That is something quite apart from an ability to explain the manner in which a phenomenon appears or can be made to perform work. Suppose Faust should ask whether the electrical engineer understands electricity in the same way a man understands hunger, or knows it the way he knows a woman? If understanding is taken to mean direct personal experience—unaided, for example, by such abstract techniques as mathematics—then Faust's longing to free himself from magic, to unlearn sorcery and to confront Nature *ein Mann allein* is a wish not alien to modern man. We have long dedicated ourselves to science out of love of God and our yearning to know and appreciate His creation. All the magic benefits which science has now showered down on us are baubles which often only frustrate that unfulfilled desire, and we feel akin to Faust at the end, blindly imagining his demons at constructive work, while they are busy digging his grave.

Nor can we restrict our practice of "magic" in this broader sense to the attainment of mere material ends and creature comforts: magic may even be implicit in "scientific method." The biologist, for example, unable to define such a fundamental concept as "species" either in time or by spatial distribution, resorts to an ununderstood criterion: production of fertile offspring. But this is a tautology. Why can two individuals interbreed?—Because they are members of the same species. Faust's insistence on final understanding in human terms would probably indict much of science as an appeal to "magic."

Older *Faust* criticism sometimes took Occultism very seriously, so that a great deal was written especially about alchemical influences and sources. The *Faust* text, on the other hand, takes alchemy lightly, as when Faust scornfully contrasts its high-flown terminology with its empty promises:

042   Da ward ein Roter Leu, ein kühner Freier,
      Im lauen Bad der Lilie vermählt
      Und beide dann mit offnem Flammenfeuer
      Aus einem Brautgemach ins andere gequält.
      Erschien darauf mit bunten Farben
      Die Junge Königin im Glas,
      Hier war die Arzenei, die Patienten starben,
      Und niemand fragte, wer genas!

      There was a Lion red, a wooer daring,
      Within the Lily's tepid bath espoused,
      And both, tormented then by flame unsparing,

By turns in either bridal chamber housed.
If then appeared, with colors splendid,
The young Queen in her crystal shell,
This was the medicine—the patients' woes soon ended,
And none demanded: who got well?

Again in Part II alchemy is employed as a prime example of bogus claims, this time in connection with inflationary currency (4955–4970).

More recent critics have been quick to see that Faust is by no means best understood as a 16th-century or a Renaissance man. Especially Marxist influence has prompted us to interpret literature as a document of its time, or even to assume that a responsible writer will show concern for issues of his own day and age. Goethe himself, however, does seem to have taken pains on various occasions to discourage precisely this sort of interpretation. There is, for example, his well-known denial that the Baccalaureus of Act I is related to Fichte's solipsistic philosophy. Similarly, he deleted Humboldt's name at 5137 in favor of a less well-known but classical botanist, Theophrastus.

Even these trivial examples show how Goethe seems to have been addressing himself to posterity as well as to his contemporaries. His success depends in large measure on the wisdom of such grand thematic choices as Humanism and Occultism, drawn by the 18th-century poet out of the 16th century and presented to us as permanent concerns of man.

III

ATTEMPT TO RETURN TO THE COMPOSITION

"Witch's Kitchen" is the only complete scene not included in the Göchhausen MS but showing up in *Faust. Ein Fragment* (1790). Now the author is a man approaching middle age, tempered by a long and exacting career as virtual head of state in Weimar. He has arrived at a time of life when he is most concerned about his own personal development, and he has somehow found the remarkable resolve to cast off his position (he compared it to a snake shedding his skin) in order to embark on an uncertain adventure as author, beginning with a two-year stay in Rome. As an artist Goethe has become acutely conscious of form and of the severe restraints it imposes.

It is a very different man who tried to take up the *Faust* MS where the stormy young anti-rationalist had left off. Why his attempt was abortive may seem obvious if we compare those works which he did successfully complete around 1790 (*Iphigenia*, *Egmont* and *Tasso*) with "dramatic" products of the early 1770's (*Götz von Berlichingen*, *Jahrmarktsfest zu Plundersweilern*). We wonder why he ever undertook such a difficult reconciliation between youth and middle age in the first place.

As we have seen from "Dedication," however, Goethe's writing had for him precisely this function of bridging time. On the very eve of his departure for Italy in the fall of 1786, he prepared that famous, highly personal novel of his youth, *Werther*, for his collected works, which he had now decided to publish; he made some small changes and additions, as he felt, in harmony with the original. His trip south and his early days in Rome were occupied by a much more thorough revision of his *Iphigenia* of 1779. He next turned to the more formidable challenge, *Egmont*. Its earliest conception reached all the way back to the period before Weimar, perhaps even to a time when parts of *Faust* were still being written. He had tried to finish *Egmont* before this (1778, 1782), but had never managed it. Hence he had good reason to be elated when he pieced the drama into final form during the summer in Rome, work of his youth and middle age so skillfully joined that none would be able to discover a seam. Should he not allow himself the hope that the *Faust* fragments might help him to explore even farther into the depths of his personal past?

He was to be disappointed. These early memories were embarrassing and distasteful to him. As an old man, when he was bequeathed some of his letters from his university days, he burned them all, "leaves from my own hand which expressed only too clearly in what pitiful moral limitations the years of my youth had been passed." He had already done exactly the same thing at least once while still in his twenties, when the burning of his letters caused "quiet reflection on my past, on our confusion, urgency, thirst for knowledge when we are young, how we go to such great lengths to find some satisfaction, how I found a special gratification in mysteries and dark, phantastic imaginings." *Faust* probably acted as an even more effective reminder of those early, most difficult years. "Witch's Kitchen" is significant for the glimpse it gives of the mental processes engaged in his resumption of work. It startles us by the great frankness with which they are displayed.

In terms of the total mood of the completed *Faust*, we have arrived at the decided low point of Part One. After the dismal "Auerbach's Tavern," where we with a taciturn Faust observed *homo insciens*, "Witch's Kitchen" makes an important contribution to the dark understructure of crude brutality and lewd sexuality which is apparently essential to the tragedy about to begin. The contrast between this leering, lurid night and the clear, Sunday morning daylight where Gretchen encounters Faust is stark, but that day does follow after—and is made possible by—this night. "Witch's Kitchen" was obviously inserted into the early manuscript for the purpose of connecting the scholar scenes to the Gretchen tragedy by making Faust young again; its deeper meaning—for Faust as for Goethe—must be sought among those ununderstood, often shameful forces in our soul which are so intimately bound up with love. "Witch's Kitchen" casts some doubt even on what Gretchen says of her own love,

585   Doch—alles, was dazu mich trieb,
        Gott! war so gut—ach, war so lieb!

        Yet—all that drove my heart thereto,
        God! was so good, so dear, so true!

and it makes abundantly clear that Faust's motivation was by no means entirely "good, so dear, so true."

"Witch's Kitchen" is especially interesting as an early example of how Goethe, in exploring depths of the psyche, came to rely on compositional principles drawn from the structure of dream. Both in waking and in dreaming we may encounter the unexpected, but it is characteristic of the dream environment to assume, as here, the phantastic color of fairy tale, in which emerge stock materials like the mirror on the wall (at 2429). Especially reminiscent of the dream is that compelling fascination which fixes our attention on objects both pleasant and repugnant. Thoughts are channelled in paths not of logic, but of traditional proverb and speech pattern:

2394   O würfle nur gleich
        Und mache mich reich
        Und laß mich gewinnen!
        Gar schlecht ists bestellt,
        Und wär ich bei Geld,
        So wär ich bei Sinnen.

        O just roll the dice
        And make me rich
        And let me win.
        Things are pretty bad
        But if I were in the money
        I'd be in my right mind.

Here the association which leads from money to mind is a linguistic one: both use the same preposition *bei*, each in a different, highly idiomatic way. The result of this associative technique is a kind of nonsense, yet it somehow seems to premise a hidden meaning which forever eludes us.

Faust's first reaction to these silly monkeys was:

2387   So abgeschmackt, als ich nur jemand sah!

        Absurder than I ever yet did see.

For a long while he falls silent, until we find him bemused by the image in the mirror. The monkey's Whorfian nonsense continues:

2454   Wir reden und sehn,
                       Wir hören und reimen—

FAUST gegen den Spiegel.   Weh mir! ich werde schier verrückt.

MEPHISTOPHELES auf die Tiere deutend.   Nun fängt mir an
    fast selbst der Kopf zu schwanken.

DIE TIERE.   Und wenn es uns glückt,
              Und wenn es sich schickt,
              So sind es Gedanken!

FAUST wie oben.   Mein Busen fängt mir an zu brennen!
Entfernen wir uns nur geschwind!

THE ANIMALS. We speak and we see,
              We hear and we rhyme!

FAUST (before the mirror).   Woe's me! I fear to lose my wits.

MEPHISTOPHELES (pointing to the Animals).   My own head,
    now, is really nigh to sinking.

THE ANIMALS. If lucky our hits,
              And everything fits,
              'T is thoughts, and we're thinking!

FAUST (as above).   My breast begins to burn
Let us go right now.

Ostensibly, Faust is reacting to what he sees in the mirror, his back
turned to the others on stage. In a play everything, including
psychic processes, must be either vocalized or mimed: this is the
monkeys' dramatic function, to project a passive Faust's inner confusion to the audience. He is affected not by *mere* nonsense, but
reacts to some maddening *sense*—or near sense—which he cannot
quite grasp and which is conveyed to us by the monkeys' doings and
sayings. Nor need *we* look for that hidden meaning. Goethe had not
read Freud. He did know the urgent longing, familiar to all of us, to
discover what is portended by the nonsense of our dreams; all he
offers us here is that nonsense, which drives us mad because we
know it hopelessly disguises some familiar meaning.

Our dreams include utterances of folk wisdom:

2402   Das ist die Welt:
        Sie steigt und fällt
        Und rollt beständig.

        The world's the ball:
        Doth rise and fall,
        And roll incessant.

There are allusions to proverb, e.g., *Glück und Glas, wie bald
bricht das:*

2405   Sie klingt wie Glas—
        Wie bald bricht das!

        Like glass doth ring,
        How soon will 't spring!

Folklore can then be used to develop a threatening gesture:

2419   Sieh durch das Sieb!
        Erkennst du den Dieb
        Und darfst ihn nicht nennen?

Look through the sieve!
Know'st thou the thief,
And darest not name him?

and the personal impact of general folk property is always retained.

There is obscenity in dreams, as between Mephistopheles and the Witch; there are images to be gazed on in deep fascination, like the reclining nude in the mirror. Some have found in this presumptive ideal beauty a reflection of the classicism which Goethe is said to have developed in Italy. I doubt that. The senseless desperation which pervades "Witch's Kitchen" helps even to refute the pious legend about Goethe's discovery of classical form in Italy, tranquil .and symmetrical. The sensuality which he encountered there may be apparent in "Witch's Kitchen," as well as the moral rejection of Italy which necessarily followed in the mind of a Protestant from Frankfurt. The years following Italy were difficult ones, a slow return to productivity. "Witch's Kitchen" in Faust's career may even be said to symbolize what Italy was in Goethe's own: an attempt at rejuvenation, certainly a crisis, an important turning point in the man's life—but an episode by no means to be evaluated solely in positive terms.

Its most delightful feature is one which is characteristic of the entire *Faust* poem, but especially obvious here. Goethe had a remarkable ability of colorful visualization and often conveyed such impressions starkly. Earliest evidence of his gift as a scenist are perhaps the magnificent battles and burning villages in *Götz von Berlichingen* (where we may become convinced that he anticipated the color film spectacular). By the Italian period, when exclusively artistic considerations became most important to him, such techniques were far advanced. In order to appreciate the color of "Witch's Kitchen," either we need a talented staging or we must be prepared to replicate Goethe's visions in our own fancy, to see the brightly costumed monkeys at their toys or, when they neglect their fire and the fuming cauldron boils over, to hear the witch come sailing down through the flame and smoke:

2465   Au! Au! Au! Au!
        Verdammtes Tier! Verfluchte Sau!

Ow! Ow! Ow! Ow!
The damned beast—The cursed sow!

Goethe had indeed managed to patch together the two main components of his old *Faust* sketches. We also have evidence of Faust's relationships to Mephistopheles and to the Earth Spirit (1770 ff. and 3217 ff.). Had he completed these starts, a *Faust* might have been produced by 1790 in accordance with its original spirit. "Witch's Kitchen" is itself evidence, however, that the poet did not manage to achieve that sympathy for his youth which would have made such a work possible. *Faust* was cast aside when he returned from Italy. Goethe had failed: he would never be able to regain the vantage point he had occupied at twenty.

About ten years later, in the late 1790's, *Faust* as a node of poignant associations out of the past did acquire significance again, as material for the new style chosen for the advancing years of his life. It is to this so-called classical period that we can now turn our attention.

IV

HELEN APPEARS

Goethe did not divide Act III into scenes with titles as such. The stage directions, "Before the Palace of Menelaus" and "Inner Court-yard of a Castle," indicate two large, unequal parts. Editors have the habit of dividing the last, larger section into two approximately equal portions, not only for the sake of symmetry but also because of the stage direction after 9573: *Der Schauplatz verwandelt sich durchaus*—"the scene is transformed entirely." Line 9573 itself,

> Arkadisch frei sei unser Glück!

> Our bliss become Arcadian and free!

introduces a marked change in tone and style.

Goethe's day did not speak of a "scene" in the modern way, but of an *Auftritt*—an "entrance" whenever characters changed. A change of scenery was not accomplished behind the lowered curtain, but by exchanging wings and backdrops, of which the typical stage had about five sets fixed at intervals from front to back. A new scene could be produced on the open stage by closing a set of wings and lowering a backdrop downstage from the players; conversely, a set of wings could be drawn back and the backdrop raised to reveal a new set directly behind the old. In this latter case all players normally had to exit before the scene change, because a transformation of scenery while the players were still standing in front of it would convey enchantment. That is what does happen after 9573. Style, tone and atmosphere, as well as stage properties, take us into a free world of fancy.

Earlier in Act III we find another point where style and atmosphere change. It is not a change of "scene" but it is—in 18th-

century terms—a new *Auftritt:* the entrance of Phorkyas at 8696.
Her presence sets off a progressing change comparable to the sudden one at 9573. At first we may notice only how Phorkyas' attitude
and then her language become more and more inappropriate to her
station, but she brings about a gradual change in Helen's bearing
and speech, too. My purpose later (Chapter IX) will require close
investigation of this change—right now I want to scrutinize only the
first two-hundred lines of Act III, those spoken by Helen and the
Chorus before Phorkyas disturbs them.

LINES 8488–8696

This material is formidable. There is little conceptual difficulty,
but many lines are hard to unravel linguistically (e.g.: 8490–93,
8531–34, 8538–40). Their obtuseness appears to be directly attributable to an artificiality of expression which at the same time lends this
section its air of pompousness. It is certainly a very serious comment
on Goethe scholarship and on German professors that this is the
Goethe whom they have often chosen to purvey to the German
people and to the world. In a crazy confusion of two distinct concepts, *classic* and *classicist,* many have referred to the great German
Klassiker and, puckering their lips in a fashion foreign to Goethe's
native speech, have chosen lines like these to chant in that elevated
funereal tone which demands that you, too, appreciate their ideal
beauty or stand condemned as a bumpkin. Clearly the most relevant
question about this part of *Faust* is: why is it so difficult and artificial?

All except the first two speeches of the Chorus and the impressive
first line *Bewundert viel und viel gescholten Helena* stems originally
from the year 1800 and hence serves as an example of the kind of
writing Goethe produced in the third and extremely important
period of *Faust's* composition. This was the era in which he envisaged a finished work along classical lines. As it turned out the Helen
Act, like *Faust* itself, was to remain a great fragment for another
generation still, completed only in Goethe's old age. It was then to
Helen that Goethe first turned his renewed efforts in 1826. When
we compare the 1800 version with what he finally printed, we discover that the original was somewhat easier to read, i.e., the older

Goethe saw fit to complicate his work further by heightening its artificiality of expression. Here are two good examples which could be substantially duplicated several times:

1800	1827

Denn Ruf und Schicksal gaben
   die Unsterblichen
Zweydeutig mir, der Schönheit
   zu bedenklichen
Begleitern. . . .

Nun aber als wir des Eurotas tiefe
   Bucht
Hineingefahren und die ersten
   Schiffe kaum
Das Land berührten, sprach
   er. . . .

Denn Ruf und Schicksal
   bestimmen fürwahr die
   Unsterblichen
Zweideutig mir, der Schöngestalt
   bedenkliche
Begleiter. . . .

Nun aber, als des Eurotas tiefem
   Buchtgestad
Hinangefahren der vordern
   Schiffe Schnäbel kaum
Das Land begrüßten, sprach
   er. . . .

Goethe did a great deal of translation during his long life, and from time to time he commented on the task. In a letter to the British translator of *Hermann und Dorothea* (May 1801), he remarked that one is confronted at the outset by a fundamental choice; either one can transfer a foreign text as far as is possible into the language, time and circumstance of one's readers (modern translators who describe language as behavior regard this as their only option), or one can ask that the reader enter into the alien cultural environment of a text which, although translated, requires him to accept an unaccustomed use of his native language. I have always felt Goethe's alternatives to be superbly exemplified in the Luther translation of the Bible as compared with the King James Version. Luther's programmatic insistence that Old and New Testament speak German like the children on the street has become proverbial. His own examples from the famous Letter on Translation offer stunning contrasts with the careful literalness of King James' scholars:

Out of the abundance of the heart the mouth speaketh.
Wes das Herz voll ist, des gehet der Mund über.

Why was this waste of the ointment made?
Es ist schade um die Salbe.

Hail Mary, full of grace.
Gott grüße dich, du liebe Marie

Since English speakers have, in time, absorbed innumerable He-
brew and Greek idioms from their Bible—"He went in unto her,"
"That is an abomination before the Lord," and the like—into their
own developing language, the end result in German and English
may be almost the same, "Biblical language" being equally familiar
to both peoples. But the ways were different. The Helen Act opens
as if it had been translated out of the Greek by King James' scholars.
Goethe did not choose to transfer Helen onto German soil. The
attempt might have done violence to Helen's identity, and the question of identity is central to Act III.

Helen is first of all a Greek, speaking not merely in classical meter
but in classical idiom as well. This makes for decidedly un-German
expressions, some even very difficult in German. Most obvious is
perhaps the unduly frequent use of participles and gerunds. Note
their concentration in the 8670's:

Nicht Schall der emsig Wandelnden begegnete
Dem Ohr, nicht rasch-geschäftiges Eiligtun dem Blick,
Und keine Magd erschien mir, keine Schaffnerin,
Die jeden Fremden freundlich sonst Begrüßenden.
Als aber ich dem Schoße des Herdes mich genaht,
Da sah ich, bei verglommner Asche lauem Rest,
Am Boden sitzen welch verhülltes großes Weib,
Der Schlafenden nicht vergleichbar, wohl der Sinnenden.
Mit Herrscherworten ruf ich sie zur Arbeit auf,
Die Schaffnerin mir vermutend, die indes vielleicht
Des Gatten Vorsicht hinterlassend angestellt.

Numerous un-German genitives as well as the free word order typical of a language more highly inflected than German contribute
further to our difficulties, compelling us to read slowly and attentively. Even the professor must pause from time to time and parse a
sentence in order to read with full comprehension.

Helen uses repeated Homericisms like "hollow ships" (8535), or ships' beaks (8539). It is natural for her to refer to the gods as the "immortals" and to make frequent allusions to Greek myth. Throughout this early portion of Act III meters are exclusively classical. When the Chorus falls into contention with Phorkyas, their stylized exchange is a borrowing from classical drama—as a matter of fact, the entire opening scene is shaped in strict accordance with classical prototypes: the setting is in the open, the figures on stage are held to a minimum.

"Hearth and home" is another Homericism, one which goes far toward circumscribing the identity of the aristocratic Greek woman of antiquity (8660, 8674, 8683). Notice the very clear organization of Helen's introductory monologue. First she explains her situation and reminds us that the spouse who has brought her here is approaching below. She closes with another reference to him, but the middle lines (8496 ff.) permit her to recall her past. She thinks of herself first of all as the scion of a specific house, speaks of her father and of her siblings. After childhood her identity continued dependent on a particular house (8502 ff.), but now on that of her husband. Only four lines refer to her desires in the present or to her plans for the future (8506 ff.); here Helen expresses her resolve to remain true to house and king, i.e., to that identity which has already emerged from her narrative.

She naturally associates Menelaus with order. She quotes him:

8555   Du findest alles nach der Ordnung stehen: denn
       Das ist des Fürsten Vorrecht, daß er alles treu
       In seinem Hause, wiederkehrend, finde, noch
       An seinem Platze jedes, wie ers dort verließ.

       All things shalt thou in ancient order find: because
       It is the Ruler's privilege, that he all things
       In faithful keeping find, returning to his house,—
       Where'er he may have left it, each thing in its place;

and again:

8569   "Wenn du nun alles nach der Ordnung durchgesehn."

"Now when all things in order thou inspected hast,"

In 8580 she even refers to him with one of those Greek participles: *der Ordnende*—"he who sets things in order." Since she understands her identity within an order established for the child by its father, for the woman by her spouse, she naturally looks on her own actions as properly an extension of her lord's ordering presence. As soon as Menelaus reaches shore he reviews his warriors:

541   "Hier steigen meine Krieger nach der Ordnung aus;
     Ich mustre sie, am Strand des Meeres hingereiht."

     "Here, in their ordered rank, my warriors disembark;
     Them shall I muster, ranged along the ocean-strand."

He commands Helen to carry out a parallel function at the palace:

549   Betrete dann das hochgetürmte Fürstenhaus
     Und mustre mir die Mägde.

     Set thou thy foot within the high-towered princely House,
     And muster well the maids, whom there behind I left.

Two important words occur in 8507: *treu* and *ziemt*—Helen is eager to carry out her king's command "faithfully," "as beseems a spouse." She is acutely conscious of who she is, and no vulgar fear shall hinder her (8604 f., 8647). The irony is obvious. Helen, who identifies herself in terms of hearth and home, suitable behavior, loyalty to her spouse and an extension of his authority, is at the same time the classical example of the woman who forsakes hearth and home to commit adultery. Her apprehension (8526 ff.) is understandable.

Her well established classical identity, however, permits Helen to enjoy a kind of security unknown to us moderns. She finds her place in a Greek order of things which lays mortal fates upon the knees of the gods. It may be that the immortals do intend her death—so be it then. On the other hand apparent, dire danger may not really portend their ill will—in that case she is safe. The all too obvious plans of Menelaus for a sacrifice and the ominous lack of any sacrificial animal are, she admits, cause for concern:

8582   Bedenklich ist es; doch ich sorge weiter nicht,
Und alles bleibe hohen Göttern heimgestellt,
Die das vollenden, was in ihrem Sinn sie deucht,
Es möge gut von Menschen oder möge bös
Geachtet sein; die Sterblichen, wir, ertragen das.
Schon manchmal hob das schwere Beil der Opfernde
Zu des erdgebeugten Tieres Nacken weihend auf
Und konnt es nicht vollbringen; denn ihn hinderte
Des nahen Feindes oder Gottes Zwischenkunft.

CHORUS.   Was geschehen werde, sinnst du nicht aus!
Königin, schreite dahin
Guten Muts!
Gutes und Böses kommt
Unerwartet dem Menschen;
Auch verkündet, glauben wirs nicht.

'T is critical; and yet I banish further care,
And let all things be now to the high Gods referred,
Who that fulfil, whereto their minds may be disposed,
Whether by men 't is counted good, or whether bad;
In either case we mortals, we are doomed to bear.
Already lifted oft the Offerer the axe
In consecration o'er the bowed neck of the beast,
And could not consummate the act; for enemies
Approaching, or Gods intervening, hindered him.

CHORUS.   What shall happen, imagin'st thou not.
Queen, go forwards
With courage!
Blessing and evil come
Unexpected to men:
Though announced, yet we do not believe.

Helen the Greek aristocrat will accommodate herself to whatever order the gods and her spouse dispose. This is what "beseems" her. All her experience since the house of her father has been determined by these higher powers. She is not who she is by her independent will or even as a consequence of events which she can comprehend:

604   Seis, wie es sei! Was auch bevorsteht, mir geziemt,
      Hinaufzusteigen ungesäumt in das Königshaus,
      Das, lang entbehrt und viel ersehnt und fast verscherzt,
      Mir abermals vor Augen steht, ich weiss nicht wie.

      Let come, what may! Whate'er awaits me, it beseems
      That I without delay go up in the Royal House,
      Which, long my need and yearning, forfeited almost,
      Once more hath risen on my sight, I know not how.

At last the Chorus raises a hymn to Helen's fatalistic philosophy
(8610 ff.).

Act III begins by focusing our attention on a firmly established
identity of Helen as Greek aristocrat in classical surroundings. She
makes every effort to conduct herself as beseems her. Phorkyas will
endeavor to shake Helen's confidence in this fixed identity and will
at last succeed, for Helen becomes unable to maintain it. In the end,
Helen's personality will return to Hades intact, however—this in
express contrast to her servants, whose beings dissolve and are
dispersed in Nature. As a consequence of our attention to Helen's
identity and our subsequent speculation about the afterlife of members of her Chorus, the larger question as to a general definition of
individual personality is introduced as a major topic in *Faust*.

The Helen fragment was conceived during that same "classical"
period which produced the rounding out of Part One into a publish-
able whole and, beyond that, envisaged the larger framework of a
great drama extending from "Prologue in Heaven" through "Burial"
with appropriate preludes and postludes. One of the latter contains
the lines:

      Des Menschen Leben ist ein ähnliches Gedicht:
      Es hat wohl einen Anfang, hat ein Ende,
      Allein ein Ganzes ist es nicht.

      The poem of man is a similar feat:
      It does begin, all right, and has an end,
      But in itself it's not complete.

Did a fundamental theme of Faust, introduced—ironically enough—at a time when the poet rejected all that is merely fragmentary, thwart its completion? Exploration of individual consciousness in quest of an answer to Helen's uncertain *welche denn ich sei*—"just which one I am," an uncertainty shared by each of us—did indeed become an inquiry which in its many variations would permeate, both prospectively and retrospectively, the entire poem. Yet if our identity is admitted to be not *ein Ganzes*, not "in itself complete," no classical frame could contain such a theme. As a consequence, further work on *Faust* was left to the ancient Goethe. He could at last approach it in the coolness and gentle irony which alone can clothe philosophical speculation in the ambivalence of poetry. If we turn to this old man now, it is not to drop the question of individual identity, for that is one of the main concerns of Act IV.

V

IMPIOUS WISDOM OF THE ANCIENT

Faust II is just about twice as long as *Faust I*. The aged author went about writing in an entirely different way than did the inspired young genius who began *Faust*, or the man in middle age who conceived but could not execute its completion. Although the old man expressed himself with unequalled succinctness and precision, the products of his seventies nevertheless seem loosely organized, and we may seek in vain for a central perception to which all is tightly related. The older Goethe became, the more contempt he showed for the world. He knew that the public would never accept *Faust II*, and he did not even plan to let them see it while he lived. He was certainly not prepared to make any concessions to our taste, and some commentators have maintained that works like *Faust II* and *Wilhelm Meisters Wanderjahre* became mere compendiums for his general wisdom and poetic reflections on a wide range of subjects.

It may be that Goethe never looked on Act IV as completed. A plot summary which he made of it as late as May 1831 implies treatment of topics only alluded to in the "finished" product. At other points we may feel that stage directions are taking the place of dialogue—as after line 10422: *Heralds are dispatched to challenge the rival emperor, etc.* It was probably to gaps such as these that Goethe returned during the final months of his life "as regards better execution of the main motifs which, in finishing, I treated all too laconically." Ostensibly, of course, Act IV has the function of introducing Faust's desire to reclaim land from the sea and build up some kind of ideal social order. Yet, from the point of view of plot, precisely how he obtained his land is unimportant. Even if we should concede the question's relevance, we would still ask why it could not be answered early in Act V—or even be anticipated far in advance by Act I. Exposition, after all, whereby the audience is apprised of events which they are not required to witness, is one of the playwright's traditional techniques.

HIGH MOUNTAINS

By Act IV the attentive reader has ceased to pay much heed to plot, anyhow, in favor of the development of thought content in *Faust II*. We have seen how Act III opens with an inquiry about identity. It then raises the questions about continuity in individual personality, and the Act closes in exploration of the effect of death on individuality. Helen returns to her classical self, Faust disappears clutching her garment, and the Chorus faces an express choice of accompanying the Queen, thus retaining their personalities in the dark underworld, or of yielding them up in order to remain among the living. Panthalis, leader of the Chorus, makes the former choice; the rest of the girls, the latter:

9981   PANTHALIS.   Wer keinen Namen sich erwarb noch Edles will,
Gehört den Elementen an: so fahret hin!
Mit meiner Königin zu sein, verlangt mich heiß;
Nicht nur Verdienst, auch Treue wahrt uns die Person.
ALLE.   Zurückgegeben sind wir dem Tageslicht,
Zwar Personen nicht mehr,
Das fühlen, das wissen wir,
Aber zum Hades kehren wir nimmer!
Ewig lebendige Natur
Macht auf uns Geister,
Wir auf sie vollgültigen Anspruch.

LEADER OF THE CHORUS.
Who hath not won a name, and seeks not noble works,
Belongs but to the elements: away then, ye!
My own intense desire is with my Queen to be;
Service and faith secure the individual life.

ALL.
Given again to the daylight are we,
Persons no more, 't is true—
We feel it and know it—
But to Hades return we never!
Nature, the ever-living,
Makes to us spirits
Validest claim, and we to her also.

These are the speculations which have been occupying us prior to
the beginning of Act IV. Similar questions are taken up after Act IV,
as well. Faust's ultimate concern in Act V is for some permanent
imprint of his personality:

583   Es kann die Spur von meinen Erdetagen
Nicht in Äonen untergehn.—
Im Vorgefühl von solchem hohen Glück
Genieß ich jetzt den höchsten Augenblick.

The traces cannot, of mine earthly being,
In aeons perish—they are there!—
In proud fore-feeling of such lofty bliss,
I now enjoy the highest Moment—this!

At last, in "Mountain Gorges," we witness the continuance of
Faust's identity beyond the grave and are assured that

104   Alles Vergängliche
Ist nur ein Gleichnis.

All things transitory
But as symbols are sent

Evidently the individual, although a momentary phenomenon on
earth, can partake of permanence. We are reminded of Goethe's
Xenion:

Nichts vom Vergänglichen, wie's auch geschah,
Uns zu verewigen sind wir ja da.

Speak not of what's transitory, however dear,
To become eternal is why we're here.

Continuity of personality is a central thematic development from
Act III through Act V. It is the function of Act IV, but especially of
"High Mountains," to relate the theme directly to Faust.

The New Testament refers to Satan as the Prince of the World.
After some ironical geological banter about the world's origins,
Bible-quoting Mephistopheles gets round to asking Faust (10129 ff.)
if there is nothing on the surface of the world he would like to
have—an explicit replay of Christ's third temptation: "The devil
taketh him into an exceeding high mountain and sheweth him all the
kingdoms of the world and the glory of them. . . ." An urbane
Mephistopheles is eager for Faust to enjoy the delights of the busy
population centers, but Faust rejects them—and for a reason at
which we ought to have a good, close look:

10155   Das kann mich nicht zufrieden stellen!
        Man freut sich, daß das Volk sich mehrt,
        Nach seiner Art behaglich nährt,
        Sogar sich bildet, sich belehrt,
        Und man erzieht sich nur Rebellen.

        Therewith I would not be contented!
        One likes to see the people multiply,
        And in their wise with comfort fed,
        Developed even, taught, well-bred,
        Yet one has only, when all's said,
        The sum of rebels thus augmented.

It is all very well that a nation grow, enjoy high standards both of
material and cultural welfare, but Faust rejects a role in all this
because he would only get rebels in the end—presumably people
who are ungrateful for, and who will finally thwart, efforts in their
behalf. Clearly, Faust's interests are not selfless ones: if his subjects
would reject him and his plans for their welfare, he has no wish to
benefit them.

Mephistopheles, in the charming condescension of a blooded
prince, recommends the sheer luxury which a productive population

offers the power structure (10160 ff.). Faust exasperates him by scorning this, too, and we find ourselves at another of those points which reveal Mephistopheles' limited comprehension of Faust's nature. The Lord referred to those limits in passing:

325   Und führ ihn, kannst du ihn erfassen,
       Auf deinem Wege mit herab—

       And if you can grasp him, lead
       Him with you on your downward course.

Faust has long since recognized them:

1675   Was willst du, armer Teufel, geben?
       Ward eines Menschen Geist in seinem hohen Streben
       Von deinesgleichen je gefaßt?

       Canst thou, poor Devil, give me whatsoever?
       When was a human soul, in its supreme endeavor,
       E'er understood by such as thou?

Here he says substantially the same thing:

0193   Was weißt du, was der Mensch begehrt!
       Dein widrig Wesen, bitter, scharf,
       Was weiß es, was der Mensch bedarf!

       How canst thou know what men beseech?
       Thy cross-grained self, in malice banned,
       How can it know what men demand?

Granted that Mephistopheles cannot understand Faust—can we, as fellow humans, comprehend his desires? Can we look into our own hearts to discover similar ones? Are we able with the same clear gaze of the aged Goethe to confess what we find there?
       When Faust says

0181   Dieser Erdenkreis
       Gewährt noch Raum zu grossen Taten,

This sphere of earthly soil
Still gives us room for lofty doing,

Mephistopheles thinks he is talking about glory. Faust denies it:

10187   Herrschaft gewinn' ich, Eigentum!
         Die Tat ist alles, nichts der Ruhm.

         Power and Estate to win, inspires my thought!
         The Deed is everything, the Glory naught.

Although he still offers no final, positive answer as to what he does
want, Faust's demand for "Power and Estate" is at least consistent
with his earlier rejection of any rule subject to the threat of rebellion. "All men," Goethe let one of his dramatic characters (a charla-
tan) say, "are egoists: only a sophomore, only a fool can want to
change that. Only he who does not know himself will deny that it is
just so within his own heart." In Act IV Faust reveals his egoistical
desire for "Power and Estate." He wants to impose his own personality by *doing*.

Act IV is late in the *Faust* poem, and very late in Goethe's life. As
any man probes about him, groping for the irreducibles in his environment, one of them is usually found to be change. He observes
that change is not a concept in any way subject to his understanding,
not an idea at all, but an experience. We experience change precisely as an impediment to our understanding, or even as a confuta-
tion of it. This was Werther's reaction:

Can you say that anything is? When everything passes, everything
rolls away like thunder, so seldom lasts through its entire potential of
existence, is alas torn away by the current, submerged and dashed
against the rocks? No moment comes which does not erode you and
your loved ones, no moment in which you are not an agent of destruction, and have to be. Your most innocent walk costs thousands,
thousands of tiny creatures their lives. . . . It is not the large sensa-
tional world catastrophes, these floods which wash away your towns,
these earthquakes which swallow up your cities, that move me. My
heart sickens at the erosive force implicit in the totality of Nature,

which has formed nothing which would not destroy its neighbor and itself. I reel with fear! Heaven and earth and all the creative powers round about me! I can see nothing but an eternally gulping, eternally regurgitating monster. (Letter of 21 August)

That outburst in 1773. Almost sixty years later the same author hit on almost the same words,

0218   Was zur Verzweiflung mich beängstigen könnte:
        Zwecklose Kraft unbändiger Elemente,

        That could frighten me to the point of desperation:
        The purposeless power of wild elements,

for expressing again the anxiety which seizes a soul in contemplation of destructive rhythms in Nature. According to the young Goethe as well as the old, there would appear to be two major features of the experience *change:* repetition of natural rhythms to no apparent end beyond the destruction and replacement of existing forms; an awful fear as the individual perceives that his own identity is also to be immersed in the general flood. The surf offers supreme illustration of both aspects in Nature (10198 ff.).

What is it that Faust wants? He hopes that he can arrest pointless change, thwart nature, the constantly gulping, constantly regurgitating monster. He has gained an advantageous insight into one great natural force: the ocean, for all its monstrous power, can yet be turned back on itself and defeated by its own most characteristic property:

0225   Geringe Höhe ragt ihr stolz entgegen,
        Geringe Tiefe zieht sie mächtig an.

        A moderate height resists and drives asunder,
        A moderate depth allures and leads them on.

Here on the Biblical "High Mountain" Faust's ultimate hope is analogous to that of Panthalis: the survival of an individual identity beyond natural limits. In his mind the question is focused on the possibility of outwitting Nature to perpetuate some one form in testimony to his having been. By Act V, the old man thinks he is about to realize that hope, even at the brink of the grave. The last we see of him on earth is at 11539 ff., where he comes forth to urge forward the work which he has pursued so ruthlessly thus far. He is still hell bent on carrying through by hook or by crook:

11551   Wie es auch möglich sei,
          Arbeiter schaffe, Meng' auf Menge!
          Ermuntere durch Genuß und Strenge,
          Bezahle, locke, presse bei!

               By whatever means are necessary
          Get workers, crowd on crowd.
          Awaken their initiative with pleasures, with austerity;
          Pay them, lure them, impress them.

His firm purpose is an imprint of his own personality which will transcend hateful change. The lovely instant of individual existence might then be commanded to linger:

11583   Es kann die Spur von meinen Erdetagen
          Nicht in Äonen untergehn.

          The traces cannot, of mine earthly being,
          In aeons perish—they are there!—

Just how is it that the fleeting instant of individuality can endure, as Faust puts it, "aeons"? In the settlement which he thinks he has established here at the brink of disaster, constantly threatened by the monstrous rhythm of the sea, in this ideal of a community which daily must conquer life and daily earn its freedom, Faust foresees an enduring society. As he has outwitted Nature by turning one of her fundamental properties (that of the sea to seek its own level) against her, he can also outwit the developmental trend of societies toward their own decline. In a constantly perilous situation the characteristic human drive to effect social change will be consumed by a daily conquering of Nature. The resulting miracle, *a permanent society*,

will owe its inception to Faust's insight of Act IV (10223 ff.), in the
last analysis to "the power of the hill" (11567).

We have been looking on Faust's end from the vantage point of
"High Mountains," asking why he wants land at the verge of the sea.
He is intelligent enough to perceive that the hundreds of thousands
who might for a time revere a sovereign and benefactor will eventually destroy what he has done ostensibly in their behalf ("The Deed
is everything, the Glory naught"—10188), thus robbing his deeds of
their essential reality: permanence. Therefore he schemes to outwit
the sterile ocean and make it his productive ally in maintaining a
society with at least one permanent feature, thus assuring that an
imprint of his own personality, his moment as an individual, will
survive. Is not this the real attraction of power (if we, with Goethe,
view the world and our own hearts with a clear, impious eye)—the
privilege of imposing our own identity, and the dream of command-
ing our fair moment on earth to linger?

81   Zum Augenblicke dürft ich sagen:
      Verweile doch, du bist so schön!

      Then dared I hail the Moment fleeing:
      "Ah, still delay—thou art so fair!"

Faust knows that the man who aspires to power in this authentic
sense must forego all else:

52   Wer befehlen soll,
      Muß im Befehlen Seligkeit empfinden . . .
      So wird er stets der Allerhöchste sein,
      Der Würdigste!—Genießen macht gemein.

              He who would command
      Must in commanding find his highest blessing . . .
      Thus will he ever be the highest-placed
      And worthiest!—Enjoyment makes debased.

The Emperor has not looked life squarely enough in the eye to
perceive such hard truths as that, the essence of power escaping him

who can be distracted by its glittering, lascivious surface. "He had his fun, and how!" (10260), thus bringing affairs of state to a pass where authority is weak, unrest widespread and empire reduced to the political axiom

10279   Herr ist, der uns Ruhe schafft!

Who gives us peace shall ruler be.

Immediately upon Faust's utterance (10233), not of his real wish yet, but merely of the first command toward its realization, Mephistopheles beckons and violence begins—you can't make an omelet without breaking eggs:

Drums and military music

In subsequent scenes Goethe delineates the archetypal emergence of order out of strife, and allegorical figures hold the stage: *vom ganzen Praß die Quintessenz*—"out of the whole batch, the quintessence" (10322).

ON THE PROMONTORY

Mephistopheles wins a decisive battle for the Emperor—and how ambiguous that word: *for!* The situation is first explained to us by two imperial spies who paint the classical picture of society in ferment: many loyal citizens inactive while relatively few threaten the status quo by violence (10389 ff.); widespread dissatisfaction congeals into rebellion with the emergence of a leader (10399 ff.). Goethe seems to be interested in reducing complex political occurrences to the simplest observations.

The emperor's ingenuous eagerness to earn his empire by test of arms (10409 ff.) calls self-seeking men like Faust and Mephistopheles to the fore. They introduce themselves candidly as sorcerers and claim to be sent by a wizard whom the Emperor once befriended (10439 ff.—a situation referred to again at 10606 ff. and 10987 ff.). Bad news from home prompts the Emperor to accept Faust's help. Bully (aggressiveness personified), Havequick (greed) and Holdfast (avarice) have something in common which becomes clear when their companion Speedbooty appears: we recognize in all of them the spirit of opportunism as it thrives in wartime.

Neither Faust nor Mephistopheles permits us any doubt as to the unconscionable measures which they will apply during the impending battle. Hence the military outcome is therefore not the point at issue here. The important battle is for the soul of the Emperor, who must first be reconciled to employing morally reprehensible tactics. His first defeat occurs when he accepts augured victory:

10638   Seis, wie gedeutet, so getan!
         Ich nehm es mit Verwundrung an.

         Even as presaged, so may it be!
         I take the sign, admiringly.

Mephistopheles immediately strikes another blow: the unhappy Emperor sees his left flank crushed (10654 ff.). Two ghostly conflicts proceed side by side, Mephistopheles waging the one within, the other without.

When the Emperor arrives at the desperate certainty that his cause has been irretrievably lost on account of his own foolish connivance with evil, he is precisely where Mephistopheles wants him: fully aware of his infernal helpers and at the same time desperate enough to commit not just folly, but a sin of calculated intent. It is the ancient game of every confidence artist to implicate his victim in guilt so the victim becomes, as an accomplice, helpless to escape. At times, the *Faust* text has even led us to believe evil impotent without human agency—as of the Witch:

2376   Der Teufel hat sies zwar gelehrt;
        Allein der Teufel kanns nicht machen.

        The Devil taught the thing, 't is true,
        And yet the Devil cannot do it.

Here, however, Mephistopheles does not merely parry while man strikes; he arrogantly demands

10692   Befehlt, dass ich befehlen darf!

        Command that I may give command!

The Emperor keeps up appearance by withholding the staff which is the outward symbol of authority, but his final capitulation is unambiguous:

10705   Befiehl und such uns zu befreien!
        Geschehe, was geschehen kann!

        Command, and try to free us
        Let the chips fall where they may.

Now Mephistopheles can in good conscience go ahead and dispose of the external battle as well, the really interesting one being over:

10710   FAUST.   Was ist zu tun?

        MEPHISTOPHELES.   Es ist getan!—

        FAUST.   What's to be done?

        MEPHISTOPHELES.   The thing is done!—

Some water spirits invade dry land so that the enemy think they are flooded. The humor of 10734 ff. is revealing. Mephistopheles' exclusively rational eye is blind to those human illusions which make up the world in which we live, even when he is responsible for them! Our behavior can appear only inordinate and ridiculous if it is a response to motivating forces which he cannot perceive—as, for example, Faust's and Gretchen's carryings on which Mephistopheles, oblivious to the cause of their agitation, thought so absurd and obscene. Here in Act IV he can see the men swimming, but can't see the water.

THE RIVAL EMPEROR'S TENT

Allegorical figures reappear, no longer to reveal true motivations of men in wartime, but now to offer an unadorned view of why a state comes to be formed: to dispense booty in an orderly fashion. We are dealing here with the wisdom of Goethe's old age. It derives in large part from his lack of piety: this scene contains the statement that legal procedures may differ from illegal ones in point of order only, not in terms of moral right and wrong. It is a point made most forcefully by St. Augustine in the *City of God:*

> ... what are bands of brigands but petty kingdoms? They also are groups of men, under the rule of a leader, bound together by a common agreement, dividing their booty according to a settled principle. If this band of criminals, by recruiting more criminals, acquires enough power to occupy regions, to capture cities, and to subdue whole populations, then it can with fuller right assume the title of kingdom, which in the public estimation is conferred upon it, not by the renunciation of greed, but by the increase of impunity.

The "Roman Elegies" hark back to a few huts on the banks of the Tiber, then

> sie vom wimmelnden Volk glücklicher Räuber belebt. Alles schleppten sie drauf an diese Stätte zusammen...

> nations enlivening hills teeming with fortunate thieves. Onto this spot they dragged up their assembled plunder...

and out of these beginnings arose the imposing political structure of Rome.

The Mighty Men and their woman, unencumbered, attain enemy headquarters first, but their simple means and unorganized condition are insufficient to avail them of their advantage. What little they do get away with is scattered as they go:

814   O weh, die Schürze hat ein Loch!
       Wohin du gehst und wo du stehst,
       Verschwenderisch die Schätze säst.

       The apron has a hole, ah woe!
       Wherever thou dost walk or stand,
       Thou sowest treasure on the land.

The balance of the scene treats the mode in which legal processes are now developed for sharing and maintaining the winnings. The Holy Roman Empire—defunct, incidentally, for almost a quarter-century at the time Goethe wrote this—is taken as an adequate allegory for all such political arrangements.

Order can be instituted by appointment of vassals, i.e., by assignment of significant shares of the spoils in recognition of important personal services to the sovereign victor. Acceptance occurs in connection with a pledge of future loyalty, while the relationship between liege lord and vassal continues to be thought of in terms of intimate personal service. Ancient Sumerian or Egyptian regimes might yield virtually the identical lesson, but Goethe preferred the provisions of the Golden Bull of Charles IV for good reason, and it is not his first allusion in *Faust* to that document. We were reminded of it as early as Act I, and then again when Helen learned of the vassals pledged to her protection. Goethe's interest was not in the Holy Roman Empire as such; it seems to have struck him as a kind of archetype for political organization of whatever specific form, because the backbone of state appeared to him to be a pact between powerful lords and their sovereign, anchored in mutual self-interest. This political philosophy can be partially explained on the simple observation that it was corroborated in those regimes with which Goethe had life-long experience. Beyond this, however, it also permits us to single out two fundamental traits of the so-called wisdom of the ancient.

On the one hand he was inclined to view the multiplicity of forms in the world about him as susceptible to interpretation in archetypes—not necessarily prototypes, from which individual forms would have to derive historically. His archetype came to be an ideal perception of interrelationship among many specific given forms. He thought, for example, that there must be some archetypal plant form to which all plants and even plant parts could be related. As a young man, he even sought to discover it among the plant kingdom: "It must exist! How else would I recognize this or that structure as a plant if they weren't all formed in accordance with one pattern?" (April, 1787). Act IV makes the assumption that there must be some archetypal political arrangement in relation to which we can best comprehend the many specific forms under which men are in fact, and have been, governed.

In his ardent effort to relate disparate phenomena to their simplest common ideal Goethe refuses to allow his gaze to be clouded by piety or by wishful thinking. He will not assume that society's political systems can be derived rationally, as from the hypothetical compact popular among some of his contemporaries. He makes instead the quite ruthless observation that sound political arrangements draw their guarantees from the self-interest of the powerful. Goethe's proclivity to view matters in such a hard way may be easier for the reader to accept here in Act IV, where the subject is politics, than in Act V, where the subject is man.

These observations on the mentality of the ancient as it is reflected in Act IV conclude our survey of *Faust*'s several periods of composition. The great mutual disparity among the various stages of composition may go far toward accounting for the universal appeal of *Faust*. It is the child of many authors—young, middle-aged as well as old; radical and reactionary; ebullient and temperate.

All men must play these many parts, and as a consequence the lives of most of us are fragmented, the youth a stranger to the man. Goethe somehow learned to use his writing, *Faust* above all, as an instrument for fusing his own personality. I expect that one of his closest friends (Knebel) had something like this in mind when he made the famous remark: "What you live is better than what you write." The implication for *Faust* is obvious: one man, Goethe, did indeed live through the several intellectual and emotional epochs recorded in this work. Its unity, if such can nevertheless be argued for it, is the unity of personality. We sense in *Faust* the identity of one who may, at last, have succeeded in making *ein Ganzes* out of a human life—something "in itself complete."

VI

THE BASIC
FICTION

When Goethe was asked in 1815 how *Faust* was to end, he replied: "I mustn't reveal that, but it is finished, you know, and very successful and grandiose, from my best time." He was referring to those years with Schiller which had led to the virtual completion of *Faust I*. The style and tone of the period (1797 ff.) can be recognized easily in the three preludes, in the Easter morning and "Study Room" scenes as well as at the end of Act V. There also survive an "Epilogue" (presumably spoken by the Comic Character) and a "Departure", the former corresponding with "Prologue in the Theater" and the other with "Dedication" in such a way as to round off a monumental work in symmetry with its beginning. Schiller referred to these opening and closing pieces as a *poetischer Reif*—a "poetic ring" to comprise the entire poem. *Faust* had at last acquired its ideal frame, which any work of art must have in order to delimit its own special reality from the rest of the world.

Unfortunately, Schiller's "ring" analogy diverts our attention from the scenes leading to the pact, and they really belong in the same context. If some sort of metaphor is helpful, then I would prefer to look on those portions of *Faust* written around the turn of the century as an arch: "Prologue in Heaven" as one riser, the final scenes as the other, with "Study Room" holding the pact as keystone. The completion of this supporting structure is what permitted publication of *Faust I* and provided at the same time a base for further building in later years. The important message of the sections in question is their smiling concession that the whole story is fiction. We are not confronted with earthly figures at all, but with an anthropomorphic "Lord" and his good angels, intruded on by a folklore devil. Did Goethe, back in his day, *believe* in these things which we have now rejected? The 18th century was even farther from accepting orthodox Christianity than is the 20th. Scholars usually observe that Goethe needed some "mythological background" and thought it might as well be Christianity. Well, what is "mythology"? To put the question bluntly, are we to take it seriously, or not?

PROLOGUE IN HEAVEN

In so far as God, the angels, and the devils are concerned, Goethe stamped fiction rather plainly as such. The ultimately sane view on our world may indeed be achieved at the point when we are able to concede that crude and primitive representations like the angels praising and the devil baiting the Lord, like the blood pact or the horrible maw of hell which little devils drag on stage at the end do correspond with "reality" just about as well as any other conception within our poor capabilities. Or shall we suppose that the representation by a modern physicist with magnitudes and minitudes which challenge his own most sophisticated mathematical abstractions, with its inability to locate a particle—or blob of energy—both in here and now, with its ultimate appeal to random shuffling of vast ranges, is within our powers to comprehend? Or shall we prefer straightforward attempts to achieve "realism" in literature—the representation, for example, of everyday objects in smudgy naturalism? In the very transience of the items chosen, and for want of meaningful bearing on Deity, man and Nature, such representations often *lack* reality. While neither Goethe nor his audience believes in the "sets and stage machinery" (234) God, angels, and devil, the questions raised by these patent fictions are real enough.

An obvious consequence of employing the most flagrant fiction to raise the most authentic questions is irony: constant insistence on viewing issues from various points of view at the same time. Nothing can be taken quite seriously, neither man nor the devil himself; but by the same token nothing is merely humorous, neither the papier-mâché Lord nor his music-box angelic choir. In a generally sardonic context, an occasional utterly humorless passage can stand out stark and ominous, as in the case of Faust's horrible curse (1583 ff.) or of some especially brutal line by Mephistopheles like

1509   Du bist noch nicht der Mann, den Teufel festzuhalten.

       You are not man enough to hold the devil.

A major advantage of irony for any author lies in its continuous challenge to his reader that he remain alert, lest he laugh out of turn or be gulled if too pious. It certainly forms a highly appropriate context for witty logic as, for example, in the definition of the devil's nature (1327 ff.) or in the formulation of subtle bets in "Prologue in Heaven" and "Study Room." The ultimate value of irony in *Faust*, however, as in most other works of great literature, remains its peculiar consonance with the world where we are, in which all important issues turn out to be multivalent. In the basic fiction of *Faust* we shall certainly discover no unambiguous "idea" or message. A poem founded in irony will with a Mephistophelian grin reply to all questions in multiple choice, all answers theoretically correct, perhaps none of them right.

The Archangels, in unwitting self-parody, set the tone for the basic fiction. Their glorious songs to the sun, the earth, and the atmosphere conclude when Gabriel and Michael chime in with Raphael's closing quatrain, making a few small changes in it. In order to capture them, I offer a literal translation:

247   Ihr Anblick gibt den Engeln   267   Der Anblick gibt den
          Stärke,   Engeln Stärke,
      Wenn keiner sie ergründen   Da keiner dich ergründen
          mag;   mag,
      Die unbegreiflich hohen   Und alle deine hohen
          Werke   Werke
      Sind herrlich wie am ersten   Sind herrlich wie am ersten
          Tag.   Tag.

      Its aspect [of the sun's   Its aspect [presumably, of
          course] gives the angels   Creation] gives the
          strength   angels strength,

Even if none can fathom it;	Since none can fathom
The incomprehensibly	Thee,
grand works	And all Thy grand works
Are glorious as on the first	Are glorious as on the first
day.	day.

However we may choose to take these little variations, the subject of the Archangels' hymn remains the "incomprehensibly grand works" of the Lord. All of us mortals have at some time felt that it is not right of Him to expect our adoration while persisting in being incomprehensible—and many of us have suspected Him of being incomprehensible for no other reason than to be the more adored (248 and 268).

This is why it is so refreshing for Mephistopheles to step up, he who dares penetrate the glistening clouds of piety which surround Creation as depicted by the Archangels, and speak in behalf of man unseen below them. Is it not our opinion to which he so eloquently gives voice? We are pleased to hear that someone is interested in us. The Archangels roll pious eyes toward the heavenly bodies and chant in harmony that all is well. We know better, and so does our clearwitted friend:

279   Von Sonn' und Welten weiß ich nichts zu sagen;
      Ich sehe nur, wie sich die Menschen plagen.

      Of suns and worlds I've nothing to be quoted;
      How men torment themselves, is all I've noted.

The Lord's gentle reproach:

295   Ist auf der Erde ewig dir nichts recht?

      Find'st nothing right on earth, eternally?

—might He not be speaking to you or to me? We are asked to believe that He loves us, but Mephistopheles sympathizes with us—and that is far less abstract, more credible:

297   Die Menschen dauern mich in ihren Jammertagen;
      Ich mag sogar die Armen selbst nicht plagen.

Man's misery even to pity moves my nature;
I've scarce the heart to plague the wretched creature.

An important source of irony for "Prologue in Heaven" is the Lord's inability to speak except in venerable saws like

317   Es irrt der Mensch, solang er strebt.

Man errs as long as he strives.

Thus he falls into a familiar, rigid pattern.

299   DER HERR.   Kennst du den Faust?

MEPHISTOPHELES.   Den Doktor?

DER HERR.   Meinen Knecht!

THE LORD.   Know'st Faust?

MEPHISTOPHELES.   The Doctor Faust?

THE LORD.   My servant, he!

Even at the time of Job this drama had already been played out countless times.

308   DER HERR.   Wenn er mir jetzt auch nur verworren dient,
So werd ich ihn bald in die Klarheit führen.

Though still confused his service unto Me,
I soon shall lead him to a clearer morning.

Is not this the ancient cliché which no religion finds too stale? An American Protestant hymn of the 1930's:

Trials dark on every hand and we cannot understand
How the Lord is going to lead us to the blessed promised land,
But he'll guide us with his eye and we'll follow till we die:

We will understand it better by and by.
By and by, when the morning comes,
When the mists have rolled away, in that land of perfect day:
We will understand it better by and by.

On earth man is exposed to the powers of evil (315 ff.), this being a
part of that ununderstood divine plan, and man's ultimate salvation
one of those "incomprehensibly grand works" which enable us to
adore the Lord. The ideas are ancient and familiar, so that the main
purpose of "Prologue in Heaven" is merely to guide us onto well-
trodden paths deftly and light-heartedly:

323   DER HERR.   Nun gut, es sei dir überlassen!
       Zieh diesen Geist von seinem Urquell ab
       Und führ ihn, kannst du ihn erfassen,
       Auf deinem Wege mit herab—
       Und steh beschämt, wenn du bekennen mußt:
       Ein guter Mensch, in seinem dunklen Drange,
       Ist sich des rechten Weges wohl bewußt.

       THE LORD.   Enough! What thou hast asked is granted.
       Turn off this spirit from his fountainhead;
       To trap him, let thy snares be planted,
       And him, with thee, be downward led;
       Then stand abashed, when thou art forced to say:
       A good man, through obscurest aspiration,
       Has still an instinct of the one true way.

Although the devil is permitted to work his worst with us here, he
can never understand us mortals, who do ultimately "perceive the
one true way." Our sympathy with Mephistopheles, like the humor
of his situation, derives in large measure from the poor fellow's
furtherance of the Divine Plan in spite of himself:

340   Des Menschen Tätigkeit kann allzu leicht erschlaffen,
       Er liebt sich bald die unbedingte Ruh;
       Drum geb ich gern ihm den Gesellen zu,
       Der reizt und wirkt und muß als Teufel schaffen.

Man's active nature, flagging, seeks too soon the level;
Unqualified repose he learns to crave;
Whence, willingly, the comrade him I gave,
Who works, excites, and must create, as Devil.

The general scheme of things thus reconfirmed, the Lord turns
back to his Archangels with an "incomprehensibly grand" command:

346   Das Werdende, das ewig wirkt und lebt,
           Umfaß euch mit der Liebe holden Schranken,
           Und was in schwankender Erscheinung schwebt,
           Befestiget mit dauernden Gedanken!

           Creative Power, that works eternal schemes,
           Clasp you in bonds of love, relaxing never,
           And what in wavering apparition gleams
           Fix in its place with thoughts that stand forever!

The specific (Platonic) contrast which He draws here between the
solid world of phenomena, unreal because none of them enjoys
more than fleeting existence in the moment, and the reality of permanent idea is a distinction as venerable in man's thinking as the
other notions which we have encountered in "Prologue in Heaven".
The high value which the Lord places on *das Werdende* and his way
of relating it to *der Liebe holde Schranken*—"The sweet bonds of
love"—gives a new, distinctly Goethean twist to the old idea. These
final words of the Lord have introduced an important philosophical
view which underlies all the rest of the *Faust* poem. Like our own
lives, the greater part of *Faust* is played out in the manifest world of
transitory, hence unreal, phenomena. Here at the beginning we are
therefore reminded that there does exist another sphere, that of
permanent idea. Also at the end:

12104   Alles Vergängliche
             Ist nur ein Gleichnis;
             Das Unzulängliche,
             Hier wird's Ereignis;

Das Unbeschreibliche,
Hier ist's getan;
Das Ewigweibliche
Zieht uns hinan.

All things transitory
But as symbols are sent:
Earth's insufficiency
Here grows to Event:
The Indescribable,
Here it is done:
The Woman-Soul leadeth us
Upward and on!

In both these passages the vital bond between our world of ephemera and that better world of idea toward which we yearn is the same: *der Liebe holde Schranken*—the love of woman.

When the arch of the basic fiction at last descends, we shall witness Mephistopheles' abject humiliation and ignominious defeat. We knew it all along. What an ass he is to make a bet with God! And yet, we do take him more seriously than the sun, moon, stars, Archangels, and Lord, all mere stage properties as ordered by the Manager. Mephisto rings true. Although his tone is one of scoffing, we agree with what he has to say—as Faust would sooner subscribe to Mephistopheles' description of him (301 ff.) than to the Lord's complacent *meinen Knecht*—"my servant." Mephistopheles confesses his fond attachment to all living creatures with a self-depreciating cat-and-mouse metaphor (321 f.—and again in "Burial": 11623 ff.). This, like his reference to his many earlier defeats (334 f.) and like his famous parting shot (350 ff.), shows that he takes a scoffing, ironical view of himself, too. The supreme irony of "Prologue in Heaven" derives from the fact that in our eyes Mephistopheles, precisely because he has a sense of humor, comes off with our sympathy and hence a triumph over the Lord. The playwright's task before the curtain rings down is to make his audience eager for it to rise again. We expect Mephistopheles to turn up in the drama on earth, and our mind leaps ahead now mainly on his account.

STUDY ROOM

The first "Study Room" brings Faust and Mephistopheles together. The second contains Faust's awful curse and the pact, that crucial keystone in the fundamental structure underlying the poem. We have observed already how a good dose of irony is inherent in this fiction. "Study Room I" lays it on thick, drawing strongly on the heavy-handed puppet-play transmission out of the 16th century: Faust encounters the devil as black dog, and they converse in the archaic four-beat measure called *Knittelvers*. An opening monologue is divided ostentatiously into strophes as Faust tries alternately to concentrate, and to cope with his unruly guest. The effect is farcical, calculated to become hilarious. When Faust in a contemplative mood (1178–85) mentions "his better soul" and "love of God," he sets the poodle to running, snorting and jumping (1186–93); he reflects on "life's source" (1201), and the poodle growls (1202). An inspired Bible interpretation (1224 ff.) moves the dog to anguished howling and finally into a horrible metamorphosis. When he finally emerges as a medieval traveling scholar we recognize, in his ability to poke fun at himself, our old friend Mephisto:

1326   Ihr habt mich weidlich schwitzen machen.

    You've made me roundly sweat

In mock furtiveness he lets it be known that hell has laws, so that negotiations may be presumed possible (1413 ff.). The height of the ridiculous is only approached with the farce of the pentagram; even after Faust has been lulled to sleep Mephistopheles maintains good burlesque spirit and for our benefit requires his minions to gnaw away the star's point before he takes his leave. And so it goes. On his return he refuses to enter (1530 ff.) until summoned thrice. The pact is perhaps the best example of standard folklore property to which he adheres pedantically despite its empty formalism in the modern context. Just at the point where we are thoroughly convinced that we shall not take these trappings seriously, Goethe knows how to accomplish remarkable effects by blending the humorous and the sinister:

707   Bedenk es wohl! wir werdens nicht vergessen.

      Consider well, we shall remember this.

      The basic fiction is not contrived *merely* for good humor. It involves us rapidly in complex relationships among God, the devil and man which have to be traced out with care. "Prologue in Heaven" told us no more than that Mephistopheles considered himself to be in opposition to the Lord, who looked upon him, however, as a useful pawn in the divine scheme (340 ff.). In reply now to Faust's question, Mephistopheles appears to be in substantial agreement with the Lord's view:

35   FAUST.   Nun gut, wer bist du denn?

      MEPHISTOPHELES.   Ein Teil von jener Kraft,
Die stets das Böse will, und stets das Gute schafft.

      FAUST.   Who art thou, then?

      MEPHISTOPHELES.   Part of that Power, not
         understood,
Which always wills the Bad, and always works the Good.

The Lord characterized the angelic sphere as positive, permanent form in the ideal (349) distinct from transitory phenomena (348). Flux in this latter sphere, "which is evolving and alive" (346), necessarily implies the passing of each individual form, so that Mephistopheles, in whom Faust recognizes the agent of annihilation (1360), is presumably essential to the Lord's scheme. John Milton assured continued familiarity with the medieval cosmology for Goethe's day and ours: out of ancient darkness and primeval chaos God created light and order. A band of His angels rose up against Him and upon their defeat allied themselves with old mother night, trying spitefully to reclaim creation from order and to return it to pristine chaos. The 20th century espouses similar, if independent notions: the unmeasured universe contains finite enclaves of material organized to a lesser or greater degree—particles into elements, elements into life and, perhaps the pinnacle of order, intelligent life. The dark reaches of space remain cold and unorganized. Furthermore, conditions requisite to order include germs of entropy: for example, life-giving radiation is a progressive breakdown of elements and return to random darkness.

1349 Ich bin ein Teil des Teils, der anfangs alles war,
   Ein Teil der Finsternis, die sich das Licht gebar,
   Das stolze Licht, das nun der Mutter Nacht
   Den alten Rang, den Raum ihr streitig macht.
   Und doch gelingts ihm nicht, da es, soviel es strebt,
   Verhaftet an den Körpern klebt:
   Von Körpern strömts, die Körper macht es schön,
   Ein Körper hemmts auf seinem Gange;
   So, hoff ich, dauert es nicht lange,
   Und mit den Körpern wirds zugrunde gehn.

   Part of the Part am I, once All, in primal Night,—
   Part of the Darkness which brought forth the Light,
   The haughty Light, which now disputes the space,
   And claims of Mother Night her ancient place.
   And yet, the struggle fails; since Light, howe'er it weaves,
   Still, fettered, unto bodies cleaves:
   It flows from bodies, bodies beautifies;
   By bodies is its course impeded;
   And so, but little time is needed,
   I hope, ere, as the bodies die, it dies!

Although we may glimpse Goethe the early historian of physics behind these lines, Faust understands Mephistopheles in Scholastic terms: the devil lost a battle in heaven, but continues his war on earth against the eternal creative force (1363 ff.). That force being love, Mephistopheles personifies hate:

1379 So setzest du der ewig-regen,
   Der heilsam-schaffenden Gewalt
   Die kalte Teufelsfaust entgegen,
   Die sich vergebens tückisch ballt!
   Was anders suche zu beginnen
   Des Chaos wunderlicher Sohn!

So, to the actively eternal
Creative force, in cold disdain
You now oppose the fist infernal,
Whose wicked clench is all in vain!
Some other labor seek thou rather,
Queer Son of Chaos, to begin!

The absurd puppet play turns out to be a remarkably clear context in which to stipulate fundamentals.

The colorful fiction remains frontstage, however. Mephistopheles wants to inveigle Faust into proposing a contract (1410 ff.). His posture caricatures the petty tradesman driving a hard bargain (1416 f.), who rubs his hands and says:

1533   Wir werden, hoff ich, uns vertragen.

I hope we'll suit each other well.

He cuts a really stunning figure (1534 ff.) of the highly sophisticated, slightly jaded worldling. Experience, he recommends, is what Faust needs, and Faust agrees wholeheartedly, so sick is he of the life of reflection:

1554   Nur mit Entsetzen wach ich morgens auf,
Ich möchte bittre Tränen weinen,
Den Tag zu sehn, der mir in seinem Lauf
Nicht Einen Wunsch erfüllen wird, nicht Einen...
Der über allen meinen Kräften thront,
Er kann nach außen nichts bewegen:
Und so ist mir das Dasein eine Last,
Der Tod erwünscht, das Leben mir verhaßt.

In very terror I at morn awake,
Upon the verge of bitter weeping,
To see the day of disappointment break,
To no one hope of mine—not one—its promise keeping...
The God, above my powers enthroned,
He cannot change external forces.
So, by the burden of my days oppressed,
Death is desired, and Life a thing unblest!

Here is a case where desperation vouchsafes sincerity: Faust, quite literally, has nothing to lose by casting his lot in with the devil. That there remains for him no other resort on earth is made abundantly clear by the magnificent curse (1583 ff.), no doubt the most comprehensive deprecation in world literature. So glorious is it that Mephistopheles' lust is aroused and he makes a premature proposition, referring only to the joys of "Auerbach's Tavern" (1637 ff.). Faust does not accept, but does proceed to dispose of the last conceivable obstacle to partnership by stating (1660 ff.) that he places no stock in an afterlife.

We have come upon the feature of *Faust* which made of it a surrogate Bible for two or three generations of Germans—and indeed for many of the educated middle class the world over. In Faust they perceived a man compelled to make do with this world and, like themselves, to renounce hope of a hereafter. German professors have even boasted that more copies of *Faust* were to be found in their World War I trenches than copies of the New Testament. This was naturally an unfortunate development for the poem, because it meant that readers had begun to seek in it the kind of inflexible truth which one expects of a divinely inspired text. To do so, they had to squint past the opalescing irony which would allow them to take nothing at mere face value. A kind of super-irony resulted, for mankind has always discovered in its devotional literature—and this is what *Faust* had become—confirmation of whatever truths they happened to be touting at the moment. For example, the middle class perceived Faust's efforts to reclaim land from the sea and build an ideally assiduous society as a noble goal and as his vindication, diligence being a middle-class ideal and sociopolitical accomplishments middle-class vindications. One thing at least is certain: those who wish to see Faust's renunciation of the hereafter as analogous to their own situation may well note that Mephistopheles is just delighted. Concentration on this life alone has its reward:

1671   In diesem Sinne kannst dus wagen.
        Verbinde dich! du sollst in diesen Tagen
        Mit Freuden meine Künste sehn:
        Ich gebe dir, was noch kein Mensch gesehn!

In this sense, canst thou venture.
Come, bind thyself by prompt indenture,
And thou mine arts with joy shalt see:
What no man ever saw, I'll give to thee.

Faust scoffs at what a devil can offer him:

678   ... hast du Speise, die nicht sättigt? hast
Du rotes Gold, das ohne Rast,
Quecksilber gleich, dir in der Hand zerrinnt?
Ein Spiel, bei dem man nie gewinnt?
Ein Mädchen, das an meiner Brust
Mit Äugeln schon dem Nachbar sich verbindet?
Der Ehre schöne Götterlust,
Die wie ein Meteor verschwindet?
Zeig mir die Frucht, die fault, eh man sie bricht,
Und Bäume, die sich täglich neu begrünen!

Yet, hast thou food which never satiates, now,
The restless, ruddy gold hast thou,
That runs, quicksilver-like, one's fingers through,
A game whose winnings no man ever knew,
A maid, that, even from my breast,
Beckons my neighbor with her wanton glances,
And Honor's godlike zest,
The meteor that a moment dances,
Show me the fruits that, ere they're gathered, rot,
And trees that daily with new leafage clothe them!

This heavy sarcasm is lost on Mephistopheles. As he earlier objected
to the constant resurgence of life, hoping for an eventual return to
eternal repose, he now suggests that Faust consider peaceful en-
joyment (1691) in addition to the "pleasures" enumerated.

It is clear that Faust is bargaining from the psychologically
superior position, not just because he has nothing to lose, but
mainly on account of his very precise assessment of just what
Mephistopheles is able to offer—while, for his part, Mephistopheles
does not fathom Faust's desires at all. Faust's formulation of the
famous bet (1692 ff.) reveals a good insight into his own drives, as
well as his justly contemptuous condescension toward the silly devil

who—quite beyond his depth now—accepts eagerly. Although line 1707 is another of Mephistopheles' dire and threatening remarks (with which he can achieve a good effect on the audience), Faust is not in the least intimidated.

He has tried more reputable, more promising, "nobler" channels of discovery—what else remains now but crass experience?

1750   Laß in den Tiefen der Sinnlichkeit
      Uns glühende Leidenschaften stillen!
      In undurchdrungnen Zauberhüllen
      Sei jedes Wunder gleich bereit!
      Stürzen wir uns in das Rauschen der Zeit,
      Ins Rollen der Begebenheit!
      Da mag denn Schmerz und Genuß,
      Gelingen und Verdruß
      Miteinander wechseln, wie es kann:
      Nur rastlos betätigt sich der Mann.

      Let us the sensual deeps explore,
      To quench the fervors of glowing passion!
      Let every marvel take form and fashion
      Through the impervious veil it wore!
      Plunge we in Time's tumultuous dance,
      In the rush and roll of Circumstance!
      Then may delight and distress,
      And worry and success,
      Alternately follow, as best they can:
      Restless activity proves the man!

He expects no joy (1765), no benefit, really, at all (1766 f.). For what it is worth, he does hope to partake of the full range of human sensations.

1768   Mein Busen, der vom Wissensdrang geheilt ist,
      Soll keinen Schmerzen künftig sich verschließen,
      Und was der ganzen Menschheit zugeteilt ist,
      Will ich in meinem innern Selbst genießen,

      My bosom, of its thirst for knowledge sated,
      Shall not, henceforth, from any pang be wrested,

And all of life for all mankind created
Shall be within mine inmost being tested.

This pact scene derives its awesomeness from the extreme of desperation which brings Faust to it. He really promises nothing except to act the way he has acted, would continue to act, anyhow:

742   Das Streben meiner ganzen Kraft
    Ist grade das, was ich verspreche.

    The promise that I make to thee
    Is just the sum of my endeavor.

Mephistopheles continues to impress us as an innocuous little fellow with an inordinately high opinion of himself, whose saving grace is his sense of humor.

BURIAL

Nowhere is the stiff medieval puppet play more apparent than when the devils lurk to snatch Faust's soul as it escapes the corpse. Broad humor descends to crude speculation (11664 ff.) as to just where the exit may occur, to mild obscenity when the devils are labeled in phallic terms, and finally to perversion in poor Mephisto's unnatural passion for the angels. The burlesque probably reaches its height when a maw of hell is dragged up and Mephistopheles peers in to desribe the horrors he discerns in its recesses. He himself admits that this travesty is out of tune with the times, not so much because of minor difficulties like those which modern medicine places in the way of soul snatching (11633 ff.), as simply because no one believes in it any more (11655). As when the fiction was first introduced, the most serious matters can be dealt with, e.g., death (11604 ff.), very beautiful visions offered (e.g., 11699), but always the blatancy of the fiction is stressed. The structure upon which the *Faust* poem relies, wherever we examine it, is burlesque nonsense, while the questions it raises strike to the most fundamental underpinnings of our beliefs.

Faust might conceivably have ended here where life normally ends, at the grave, its meaning uncertain, fundamental questions about the survival of personality unanswered. In so far as the basic fiction goes, one might then argue that Mephistopheles lost his bet with the Lord but outwitted Faust. We could have no quarrel with Goethe, since his fiction would thus continue realistic: all our lives culminate in precisely this ambiguity.

A wilderness: Nature perceived at her most desolate is well disposed toward man. There are caverns for shelters; the beasts are mute, like the lions which Daniel confronted. We are looking on Nature redeemed.

The first speaker is soaring upward and downward; a second voice arises from below; a third is in a middle region. We follow a chorus of infants ("Blessed are the poor in spirit, for theirs is the kingdom of heaven") on their upward career until at last with them we find ourselves among angelic ranks. The final lines lead our mind's eye on upward and outward to infinite heavenly vistas, in much the same way as the cupola of a baroque church lavishly decorated to convey divine love on an emotional basis.

Goethe once compared religion with a tetrahedron, having four correlated aspects. In the order of their emergence as religion develops, he named them cult, dogma, ethics, and mysticism. The last and noblest of these may need some clarification, although our era is certainly acquainted with mysticism at least derivatively. Romeo and Juliet's union, John Donne with his universal love-death themes, even the pansexualism of D. H. Lawrence draw on the great tradition of European mysticism.

Fundamental to mysticism is the notion that it is possible for an individual to experience the entirety of the world, which is God, directly. Such experience passeth understanding and also defies ordinary forms of expression, so that mystics have felt themselves obliged to communicate in metaphorical terms. Traditionally, their most effective analogy for union with deity has been union in love. Mystics like to compare love with death and to discover in the similarities of the two experiences the essential qualities of true mystical union. Material for mystic symbolism derives in large part

from the Bible, especially from the Song of Solomon and from Jesus'
parables. Expressions like heavenly bridegroom and lover of the
soul (from the famous Wesley hymn) are contributions made by
mystics to stock English vocabulary.

A fine example of mystical imagery is that used by Pater
Ecstaticus (11854 ff.). All of these extreme expressions for heat,
penetration, and self-immolation are prevalent in mystical literature. Perhaps most familiar are the arrows (11858) on account of the
writings of Saint Theresa of Avila in the late 16th century. Her
description of her heavenly visitor, who repeatedly pierced her
breast with arrows, became especially well known because the Italian sculptor Bernini used her ecstatic figure to produce a most
celebrated piece of baroque sculpture.

It is appropriate for Pater Profundus to lay an intellectual basis for
mysticism. He finds it in omnipotent love that shapes and nurtures
all (11872 f.), and he argues that each of Nature's motions should
serve man's cold, impotent intellect as a reminder of that fundamental force. It now becomes Pater Seraphicus to enunciate the educa-
tive, developmental function of love in—as one example, presumably, among many—the career of the infants (11890 ff.). It is in the
company of these wee entelechies, undeveloped on earth because of
their early death, that Faust appears, to be guided with them upward by love toward God (see esp. 11918 ff.).

It was obvious at the end of "Burial" that Mephistopheles had lost
out, but we had to guess why. Here the angels explain how Faust
could be saved. They tell us nothing new: the idea that salvation
comes from above (11938 f.) is at least as old as Jewry; the com-
plementary belief that our efforts here below are related to an afterlife (11936 f.) goes back much further. As is appropriate in the
Christian terms of "Mountain Gorges," divine love receives special
emphasis as Grace:

11938   Und hat an ihm die Liebe gar
         Von oben teilgenommen,
         Begegnet ihm die selige Schar
         Mit herzlichem Willkommen.

         And if he feels the grace of Love
         That from On High is given,

The Blessed Hosts, that wait above,
Shall welcome him to Heaven!

The dogmatic terminology, "good works" and "Grace," is matched
in *Faust* with expressions like "striving" and "love." The former
principle is effective in our earthly life, but love is the force which
binds heaven to earth. This is why mystical imagery has become so
important in the final scene: mysticism alone offers a point of view
which prefers to recognize no fundamental distinction between
earthly and divine love, but rather stresses their kinship. In 11942
ff. we learn where those roses came from which the angels scatter on
Mephistopheles and raise such eruptions on his skin: from offerings
by repentant lovers to the Virgin Mary (cp. 3587 ff.).

Here is, no doubt, an element which gives our era special difficulty. In a highly civilized, enlightened day we sometimes feel that
we have left behind us the dark threat of Absolute Evil. As a consequence, *sin* ceases to be a very authentic concept in our minds.
When this is the case, we are also unable to appreciate *atonement*,
hence the "loving-holy penitents" of 11943 become merely poetic
figures. What have these young women to repent? We doubt that
they have done any serious wrong. We disagree with the most
exalted of the mystics (the bearer of the Virgin's own name), for we
do not worship Mary (12005 ff.), we do not believe in the Virgin
Birth, we do not believe very much in virgins. Certainly the word
"seduced" is long gone from our usable vocabulary. We cannot be
expected to understand

12020   Dir, der Unberührbaren,
         Ist es nicht benommen,
         Daß die leicht Verführbaren
         Traulich zu dir kommen.

         Thou the Immaculate
         Hast the power
         Drawing those who were easily seduced
         To you in hope.

Even if we could make our way back to the Victorian notion of
"seduction," we are still not prepared to agree that being seduced is

a sin, that a seduced girl needs salvation on that account—and here
we are expected to believe that she is "hard to save" (12025)! We
don't know what "lust's slave" (12027) means outside the covers of a
pulp magazine or a movie for the skin trade, and the idea of "slipping" in the moral sense of 12028 f. went out with Jonathan Ed-
wards:

)24   In die Schwachheit hingerafft,
        Sind sie schwer zu retten:
        Wer zerreißt aus eigner Kraft
        Der Gelüste Ketten?
        Wie entgleitet schnell der Fuß
        Schiefem, glattem Boden!
        Wen betört nicht Blick und Gruß,
        Schmeichelhafter Odem?

        In their weakness fallen at length,
        Hard it is to save them:
        Who can crush, by native strength,
        Vices that enslave them?
        Whose the foot that may not slip
        On the surface slanting?
        Whom befool not eye and lip,
        Breath and voice enchanting?

Just for the time being, however, let us accept the old ideas of sin,
redemption, purity, lust, etc., much as we have accepted archaic
Mephistopheles with his fat devils of the short straight horn and thin
devils of the long crooked horn for as long as they were on stage. It
all goes to make up the basic fiction of the *Faust* poem. At times this
patent fiction may correspond in an uncomfortable way with all too
recently rejected doctrines. Let us nevertheless go ahead and,
within the framework of the poem, accept the fiction of chastity and
the obligation which it implies for man and woman, the fiction that
Gretchen when seduced imperiled her soul, the fiction that mankind is characterized by fundamental, original sinfulness as well as
by a redeeming capacity for love.

Within the framework of this fiction we can appreciate the overriding importance of womankind in Faust's career: love cleanses the
sinner.

11957   Er ist nicht reinlich.
         Wenn starke Geisteskraft
         Die Elemente
         An sich herangerafft,
         Kein Engel trennte
         Geeinte Zwienatur
         Die innigen beiden:
         Die ewige Liebe nur
         Vermags zu scheiden.

         He is not pure.
         When every element
         The mind's high forces
         Have seized, subdued, and blent,
         No Angel divorces
         Twin-natures single grown,
         That inly mate them:
         Eternal Love, alone,
         Can separate them.

Woman having sinned in love, hence woman repentant, becomes in
this way the dominant theme of "Mountain Gorges," so that rhyme
and meter begin to lift Gretchen back to the surface of our consciousness (12032 ff.). We are not surprised when she comes forward
now along with famous harlots of old, echoing her prayer of 3587 ff.:

12069   Neige, neige,
         Du Ohnegleiche,
         Du Strahlenreiche,
         Dein Antlitz gnädig meinem Glück!
         Der früh Geliebte,
         Nicht mehr Getrübte,
         Er kommt zurück.

         Incline, O Maiden,
         With Mercy laden,
         In light unfading,
         Thy gracious countenance upon my bliss!
         My loved, my lover,
         His trials over
         In yonder world, returns to me in this!

Mary, now *Gloriosa* instead of *Dolorosa,* reigns in these regions:

2094   Komm, hebe dich zu höhern Sphären!
         Wenn er dich ahnet, folgt er nach.

         Rise, thou, to higher spheres! Conduct him,
         Who, feeling thee, shall follow there!

The Chorus of Mystics concludes the poem with that idea familiar
since "Prologue in Heaven": a clear distinction between a transitory
world of phenomena and a permanent one of idea.

2110   Das Ewigweibliche
         Zieht uns hinan.

         The Woman-Soul leadeth us
         Upward and on!

When Goethe's *Faust* is viewed as we have viewed it here,
through the basic fiction, it becomes a kind of Everyman drama.
Here below man does his best, impelled by a divine fire within but
entrammeled by evil circumstance and by no means pure in his
heart. He can at last be redeemed if he has striven according to his
own best lights, because a living bond of love holds his miserable
world fast to the real one. When viewed through this "poetic ring"
that comprises his adventures, Faust himself can be regarded as
representative of man, of western man, of modern man, or what
have you. Precisely because the ring is poetic it invites the reader to
endless speculation and may lull him into forgetting that it was
offered only as an artistic device.

If we choose to ask what the main issue of *Faust* is, we will not
expect an unambiguous answer to arise from material presented in
deliberate irony. It is, no doubt, essential to recognize that the
poem is not in its entirety concerned solely with Everyman and his
relationship to the hereafter. The basic fiction aside, *Faust*'s central
issue appears to be Individual Man's specific identity. Goethe was
quick to note that this topic includes, among many other considerations, man's personality in the hereafter, for a close examination of
the individual lot does betray certain intimations of immortality.

VII

THE PILGRIM SOUL ON ALIEN GROUND

LINES 606–807

That presumably tangible soul which Mephistopheles and his devils hope to catch slipping out of the navel—or wherever—is a part of the basic fiction of *Faust*. This is not to say that the poem assumes the *idea* of a soul to be fiction. It is probably good to allow a few pages for the discussion of this particular assumption as it is made by the *Faust* poem.

When Goethe returned to where his old manuscript broke off after Wagner's exit (606), he added—among other things—two hundred lines which take Faust to the brink of suicide and back in a kind of repetitive spiral. Repetitive, because Faust had already been saved from despair by Wagner's intrusion, just as the intrusion of Easter music draws him back from suicide. The Earth Spirit forced on Faust the same recognition which he contemplates anew in the lines after Wagner's exit: individual man, precisely because he has the possibility of reflecting about Nature, cannot also experience her directly. Being and transcending at the same time is denied us limited humans. Faust, therefore, paints death, the only exit from his restricted situation, in beautiful metaphor (699 ff.). From his point of view a resolute seizure of death's opportunity appears to be a worthier culmination than passive acceptance of its coming. The organization of his lyric outburst (720 ff.) is superb. The same chords touched on in preparing for suicide vibrate in subsequent lines to prevent the step. The "glass of crystal purity" (720) reminds Faust of his youth and childhood faith; he recalls the goblet's specific position in a world of venerable custom, and it is a tradition-bound Faust who then cannot take the final draught. Even the natural lyricism of the song to suicide, which rises in a "festive high salute to coming morn" (736) constitutes a transition to the hymns of the Church Pageant (737 ff.)—and Faust is back in a situation analogous to that when Wagner left. Goethe's purpose in filling out "Night" beyond Wagner's exit, if the plot has merely spiraled back on itself, cannot have been to advance the action. The importance of these lines lies in their own content: a first, tentative inquiry about *das ungewisse Menschenlos*—"the uncertain lot of man."

Individual existence implies terrible isolation. There is none to instruct us (630). Can we rely on our own impulses (631)? Whose are those impulses? The self is defined, i.e., delimited by whatever we have done and whatever has been done to us (632 f.). We have become individual by undergoing some specific development, and that has meant foregoing, one after the other, potential developmental options. When the last avenue of divergence, when our last alternative promise has been passed by, our individuality may be said to be fully matured.

So far, i.e., down to 634, Faust's reflections permit rendering into everyday prose. What now follows is more difficult. His notion that the soul (*das Herrlichste, was auch der Geist empfangen*) gets contaminated in an alien world, so that our very progress here below implies looking on the better world as "deception and delusion" while our "noble feelings" wither, is an attitude familiar to many as Romantic. Indeed the most celebrated lines in English concerning the provenience of the soul may be those which Wordsworth must have written at about the same time when Goethe was finishing out "Night":

> Our birth is but a sleep and a forgetting:
> The soul that rises with us, our life's star,
>   Hath had elsewhere its setting,
>   And cometh from afar:
>   Not in entire forgetfulness,

> And not in utter nakedness,
> But trailing clouds of glory do we come
>   From God, who is our home:
> Heaven lies about us in our infancy!
> Shades of the prison-house begin to close
>   Upon the growing boy,
> But he beholds the light, and whence it flows,
>   He sees it in his joy;
> The youth, who daily farther from the east
>   Must travel, still is Nature's priest,
>   And by the vision splendid
>   Is on his way attended;
> At length the man perceives it die away,
> And fade into the light of common day.

Although Goethe, too, seems to have done some speculating about pre-existence, these notions are not so germane to our present discussion as is Wordsworth's help in appreciating a now not so popular perception of the soul: that one attribute of man which is real, being permanent. Although it is true that we never experience an unmixed perception, or even a simple phenomenon, still it is possible in the realm of idea to imagine the unmixed, to conceive of purity: purity is the fundamental attribute of the soul as Goethe's day still commonly understood it. The soul is precisely that part of us which is not of this earth. It "cometh from afar... trailing clouds of glory... from God who is our home," but that pure essence is immediately contaminated by alien soil:

634   Dem Herrlichsten, was auch der Geist empfangen,
      Drängt immer fremd und fremder Stoff sich an;
      Wenn wir zum Guten dieser Welt gelangen,
      Dann heißt das Beßre Trug und Wahn.
      Die uns das Leben gaben, herrliche Gefühle,
      Erstarren in dem irdischen Gewühle.

      Some alien substance more and more is cleaving
      To all the mind conceives of grand and fair;
      When this world's Good is won by our achieving,
      The Better, then, is named a cheat and snare.

The fine emotions, whence our lives we mould,
Lie in the earthly tumult dumb and cold.

Romantic thinking placed understandable emphasis on childhood
as an epoch of relatively greater purity—Wordsworth again:

> O joy! that in our embers
> Is something that doth live,
> That nature yet remembers
> What was so fugitive!
> The thought of our past years in me doth breed
> Perpetual benediction.

Precisely the experience that in his "embers is something that doth
live" can save Faust from suicide, for in him, too, the memory of
childhood breeds "perpetual benediction":

71   Sonst stürtzte sich der Himmelsliebe Kuß
      Auf mich herab in ernster Sabbatstille;
      Da klang so ahnungsvoll des Glockentones Fülle,
      Und ein Gebet war brünstiger Genuß;
      Ein unbegreiflich-holdes Sehnen
      Trieb mich, durch Wald und Wiesen hinzugehn,
      Und unter tausend heißen Tränen
      Fühlt ich mir eine Welt entstehn.
      Dies Lied verkündete der Jugend muntre Spiele,
      Der Frühlingsfeier freies Glück;
      Erinnrung hält mich nun mit kindlichem Gefühle
      Vom letzten, ernsten Schritt zurück.

      Once Heavenly Love sent down a burning kiss
      Upon my brow, in Sabbath silence holy;
      And, filled with mystic presage, chimed the church-bell slowly,
      And prayer dissolved me in a fervent bliss.
      A sweet, uncomprehended yearning
      Drove forth my feet through woods and meadows free,
      And while a thousand tears were burning,
      I felt a world arise for me.
      These chants, to youth and all its sports appealing,
      Proclaimed the Spring's rejoicing holiday;

And Memory holds me now, with childish feeling,
Back from the last, the solemn way.

The Romantic idea of the soul derived of course from orthodox Christianity. The Gospel as interpreted by the Choir of Apostles depicts the soul as in exile:

791   Ach, an der Erde Brust
       Sind wir zum Leide da!

       We are upon earth's breast
       To suffer a while.

The Resurrection is promise of return out of the world:

797   Christ ist erstanden
       Aus der Verwesung Schoß!
       Reißet von Banden
       Freudig euch los!

       Christ is arisen,
       Out of Corruption's womb:
       Burst ye the prison,
       Break from your gloom!

Since Christ arose from the same earthly bonds, man can himself look toward return to unfettered, permanent existence in "God who is our home."

Goethe's lucid grasp of psychology appears at times startlingly modern, anticipating many discoveries of 20th-century psychotherapy. It is important therefore for us to remember that to him the *psyche* was still the *soul*. Modern advances in quantized description of the psyche could occur only after haunting questions such as whence and whither were dismissed as unanswerable in scientific terms, and then often forgotten as well. The older concept of a soul was anchored in faith in permanence, as distinct from this obviously unreal world in which we sojourn for a limited time.

The immediate continuation of the poem plunges Faust into those superficial experiences which the world affords; their nature and meaning, if any, for the individual are analyzed and evaluated. We have to remember that it is a soul undergoing these experiences, not a mere psyche. As alien material—*fremd und fremder Stoff*—these experiences will intrude on a being which has its proper existence in another realm.

The bet in Heaven, which presumably leads to the experiences on earth, is not at all clear. Mephistopheles cries out

312   Was wettet Ihr?

     What will you bet?

We can, if we like, take his outburst as a reply to the Lord's statement:

308   Wenn er mir jetzt auch nur verworren dient,
      So werd ich ihn bald in die Klarheit führen

     Though still confused his service unto Me,
     I soon shall lead him to a clearer morning.

There are perhaps other ways of understanding the exchange, but this one has the merit of simplicity: the Lord and Mephistopheles make a bet as to who is going to get Faust's soul when he dies—will the Lord soon lead the soul into "clarity" (309), or Mephisto gently down his path (314)? But how is the bet to be decided? On what does Faust's destiny depend? At this admittedly crucial point we ought not be too exacting. If we consider the *Faust* text as a whole, we may have to conclude that the arrangements are not quite fair. Mephistopheles, in good faith, devotes much time and devotion to his task, but loses its reward because the Lord has had a thumb on the scales, His divine love working for Faust all along:

1938   Und hat an ihm die Liebe gar
      Von oben teilgenommen....

     And if he feels the grace of Love
     That from On High is given....

Although the bet is neither precisely formulated nor entirely equit-
able, we can still make one firm observation about it: the quality of
Faust's temporal existence is conceded by both sides to be of great
significance. Mephistopheles refers to life on earth when he asks

312   Was wettet Ihr? den sollt Ihr noch verlieren,
       Wenn Ihr mir die Erlaubnis gebt,
       Ihn meine Straße sacht zu führen!

       What will you bet? There's still a chance to gain him,
       If unto me full leave you give,
       Gently upon my road to train him!

and the Lord replies:

315   Solang er auf der Erde lebt,
       Solange sei dirs nicht verboten.

       As long as he on earth shall live,
       So long I make no prohibition.

The *Faust* text appears to offer us no capability of defining the bet
any more sharply. It is true that the Lord continues:

328   Ein guter Mensch, in seinem dunklen Drange,
       Ist sich des rechten Weges wohl bewußt.

       A good man, through obscurest aspiration,
       Has still an instinct of the one true way.

while Mephistopheles contends:

334   Staub soll er fressen, und mit Lust.

       Dust shall he eat, and with a zest.

—but these two conditions are by no means mutually exclusive. All
of us know from our own experience that a man can "eat dust,"
indulge in the crudest and most brutal pleasures "and with zest,"
yet still be aware of "the one true way." Or does Mephistopheles,

unable fully to grasp mankind, in his innocence suppose that these two conditions *are* mutually exclusive—has he been outwitted so soon? Perhaps. There is really no point in our being legalistically pedantic about candid fiction, and it might just cause us to miss the real point, that *the purpose of the bet was accomplished as soon as it focused our attention on Faust's temporal existence.* For Goethe to answer all our questions, even to formulate them with any precision, would not be conducive to arousing our curiosity—and that is what his prologue is for. The audience needs to understand no more than that Faust's days on earth are in some way important, perhaps even decisive, in an eternal struggle for his soul.

This enables us to make a generalization about *Faust:* one of its themes is a questioning of the ultimate value to man's soul of direct experience in this world. Faust's famous opening monologue rejects as all too theoretical the kind of study to which he has devoted his life so far. Goethe's early work trailed off into harsh ridicule of remote, inexperienced Wagner, Faust himself not having yet attained to a more direct mode of understanding, either. Goethe's first addition to the Göchhausen Manuscript appears to have begun with Faust's strong statement of determination to seek such a direct mode of first-hand experience:

770   Und was der ganzen Menschheit zugeteilt ist,
      Will ich in meinem innern Selbst genießen,
      Mit meinem Geist das Höchst- und Tiefste greifen,
      Ihr Wohl und Weh auf meinen Busen häufen
      Und so mein eigen Selbst zu ihrem Selbst erweitern.

      And all of life for all mankind created
      Shall be within mine inmost being tested:
      The highest, lowest forms my soul shall borrow,
      Shall heap upon itself their bliss and sorrow,
      And thus, my own sole self to all their selves expanded.

Here lies the common ground on which Faust and Mephistopheles can find their basis for negotiation: both have an interest in worldly experience. Mephistopheles (like a monk) believes it will be degrading for the soul:

334   Staub soll er fressen, und mit Lust.

       Dust shall he eat, and with zest.

Faust himself places no great stock in experience. His heavy sarcasm (1675 ff.) shows that he is undeceived about the emptiness of what he is bargaining for, but he does ask for it—and quite explicitly (1750 ff.). Mephistopheles is delighted with the bargain:

1860   Den schlepp ich durch das wilde Leben,
       Durch flache Unbedeutenheit.

       Dragged through the wildest life, will I enslave him,
       Through flat and stale indifference.

Is he right? Is all we have here in this world "flat and stale indifference"? Is it only dust that we, like the serpent, eat—and like it? *Faust* focuses on "the uncertain lot of man" here below, asking the question: are our lives meaningless? We are not able to assume that Faust's ultimate salvation answers the question. "Mountain Gorges," like "Prologue in Heaven," is mere fictional framework. Granted, it is a fiction specifically designed to focus inquiry on our earth and our life, both at the poem's beginning:

1660   Das Drüben kann mich wenig kümmern...
       Aus dieser Erde quillen meine Freuden,
       Und diese Sonne scheinet meinen Leiden:

       The Beyond concerns me little
       My pleasures spring from this earth
       And this sun shines upon my sorrows.

and at the end:

11442 Nach drüben ist die Aussicht uns verrannt;
       Tor, wer dorthin die Augen blinzelnd richtet.

       The view beyond is barred immutably:
       A fool, who there his blinking eyes directeth.

Still, the deep irony of all these scenes, especially of the final ones, precludes our seeking philosophical or religious answers from them. We can conclude only that the topic of *Faust* pertains to the meaning, if any, of experience on earth for an individual soul. The author seems to have made the assumption that a great work of literature exists to raise questions, not to answer them.

VIII

INNER
DEPTHS OF
PERSONALITY

LINES 3217–39 (FOREST AND CAVERN)

The fine nature poem which introduces "Forest and Cavern" is the song of a scientist, expecially of the naturalist Goethe as we know him from his middle thirties. We could read it, if we liked, as entirely unrelated to *Faust*, an independent nature lyric giving expression to the poet's own scientific drive. In this one respect we might indeed contend that Goethe had lent Faust a bit of his own personality—but is not the urgent need for personal contact with the natural world something which Goethe and Faust share with the rest of us? Well, perhaps not. As the 20th century approaches its close, many of us have been effectively cut off from contact with natural forms. Certainly the study of nature, science, is in our minds largely associated with notions of method as taught in the schools. Science has become omnipresent and routinized to an extent that we may need to be reminded of the passionate few who, like Goethe, were devoted to it in the 18th century.

It is a fundamental quality of great lyrics that the singer in pouring out his own heart satisfies a general desire of mankind to express similar feelings. Just as 3217–39 is not the exclusive property of Faust, but belongs to all who know his need for Nature, the "Spirit Sublime" is not appropriately construed in a narrow way as a spirit who has appeared to him but to no other man. We should be off on the wrong track of a fundamental misunderstanding if we assumed that the Spirit had given Faust something which is not given all mankind, just as we fail to appreciate Faust's aspirations if we take them to be radically different from what all men seek. The "Spirit Sublime" is probably the same as the Earth Spirit (481 ff.) all right, an immanent deity, all-permeating spirit of Nature manifest in rocks, weeds, dumb animals and in ourselves.

Faust expresses our thanks for the awareness that we are a part of Nature:

3220   Gabst mir die herrliche Natur zum Königreich,
Kraft, sie zu fühlen, zu genießen,

Thou gav'st me Nature as a kingdom grand,
With power to feel and to enjoy it.

Detached observation is an essential ingredient of scientific method. To observe Nature solely from this point of view of one alien to her, however, is to forego the participation essential to genuine understanding. Faust thinks that his powers of observation are quite as sharp as those of "cold astonishment," but deeper, too:

3221   Nicht
Kalt staunenden Besuch erlaubst du nur,
Vergönnest mir, in ihre tiefe Brust
Wie in den Busen eines Freunds zu schauen.
Du führst die Reihe der Lebendigen
Vor mir vorbei und lehrst mich meine Brüder
Im stillen Busch, in Luft und Wasser kennen.

Not only cold, amazed acquaintance yield'st,
But grantest, that in her profoundest breast
I gaze, as in the bosom of a friend,
The ranks of living creatures thou dost lead
Before me, teaching me to know my brothers
In air and water and the silent wood.

An observer of the natural world who applies not only his sharp intellect but also appreciation of his own kinship to this environment discovers that in contemplation of Nature he is learning about himself:

3233   und meiner eignen Brust
             Geheime, tiefe Wunder öffnen sich.
             Und steigt vor meinem Blick der reine Mond
             Besänftigend herüber, schweben mir
             Von Felsenwänden, aus dem feuchten Busch,
             Der Vorwelt silberne Gestalten auf
             Und lindern der Betrachtung strenge Lust.

             Then show'st me mine own self, and in my breast
             The deep, mysterious miracles unfold.
             And when the perfect moon before my gaze
             Comes up with soothing light, around me float
             From every precipice and thicket damp
             The silvery phantoms of the ages past,
             And temper the austere delight of thought.

It is as if both Freudian and Jungian convolutions were crammed into a single nutshell—the individual personality in terms both of its inner depths and of its cultural background. In this chapter and the next I want to pursue Goethe's thinking on each of these subjects.

First, however, just a brief excursion to stress a way in which Goethe differs most strongly from modern psychology insofar as I am acquainted with it. For want of a better word I will call it Goethe's *synthetic* way of looking at the world. The 22-line poem we have been discussing is very lyrical, i.e., it is an especially direct form of expression. Its concern, as is appropriate for a lyric, is with the individual personality. It makes the assumption that a major source of information and even a fundamental mode of understanding for this topic lies in the area of the biological and physical sciences—in that study which used to be called natural history. "Natural history" is an unfashionable term for us, who have long since come to take it for granted that the man who would arrive at a basic understanding of almost any subject must specialize in it, certainly focus his intellectual powers more sharply and intensely than broad fields like botany, zoology, geology, astronomy indicate. Each premises mathematics, chemistry, physics and includes numerous more specialized studies like microbiology, molecular spectroscopy—and still I am mentioning areas larger than any budding scientist can choose as his own field of expertise.—Now here is Goethe, not only so old-fashioned that he regards all of natural history as one rewarding field of inquiry; he is clearly including psychology in that general topic and relating cultural history to it as well! Are we not happy that he chose a lyric as his medium in which to mix things up in that way? Far be it from us to consider anything in a lyric poem relevant to serious scientific endeavor.

By and large when we are dealing with literary documents, particularly with ones from eras other than our own, one of the correct questions is: where does the documented mentality differ from our own? We have here come upon one answer as pertains to Goethe. Our own mentality normally assumes that some degree of specialization is necessary for any respectable study. Goethe assumes that only as a consequence of synthesizing observations with a broad scope are we likely to learn anything really worth knowing. Thus, to him, specialization would *preclude* significant discovery. It is true that we are dealing with Goethe in his most vigorous research years. The old man finally resigned himself to the epoch of specialization and to the humdrum level of discovery which it seemed to promise.

WALPURGIS NIGHT

Analysis is not objectionable so long as we remember its limitations. I want to analyze "Walpurgis Night": I may cut it up wrong, but we can at any rate have a closer look at the pieces, be they organic parts or merely arbitrary fragments. One obvious division is that between "Walpurgis Night" and "Walpurgis Night Dream." Furthermore, some organizational lines seem apparent within "Walpurgis Night" itself.

3835–3955. There is an introduction, in which Faust and Mephistopheles pass through wild regions on their way to the Brocken, a Will-O'-The-Wisp as their guide. The three fall into a kind of operatic dialogue (3871 ff.). When they arrive on the mountain they describe it in surrealistic terms.

3956–4075. Arrived, Mephistopheles and Faust are for a time surrounded by crowds. Witches come sailing by. Faust and

Mephisto have trouble moving about. Faust wants to press on to the
midst of things, but Mephistopheles pulls him to the sidelines (4025
ff.), and Faust yields unwillingly (4037 ff.).

4076–4222. At last individual figures command the scene. Public
personalities like a General, a Prime Minister, etc., are treated
satirically, but a witch peddling fundamental instruments of power
gives things an ominous turn. More serious yet is she whom
Mephistopheles calls "Lilith, Adam's first wife." Two obscene dancing witches prove interesting, but an enlightened individual denies
their existence. In dancing with the pretty one, Faust must witness
a very shocking event: a red mouse jumps out of her mouth. Something else may happen, too, but before he can tell about it the
Gretchen figure distracts him. Mephistopheles makes light of the
apparition and then announces the Intermezzo "Walpurgis Night
Dream."

Our survey appears to reveal an overall organizational intent:
down through the Gretchen phantom the degree of significance of
the objects and figures is progressively heightened. All mean something to Faust, but each successive encounter strikes to a yet deeper
level of his psyche. The concluding three episodes might be taken to
illustrate my point. After the gay sexuality of the young witch, the
red mouse harks back to earliest masculine apprehensiveness about
womankind in general, and at last the prophetic vision of Gretchen
embodies Faust's deepest fears about that particular woman who
concerns him most. Even our daytime intellect recognizes an interrelationship among these three impressions; in the depths of our
awareness we apprehend an ineffably profound consonance of
theme. Woman is perceived as a threat to the stability of the masculine personality.

There seems to be something incongruous about the choice of the
title *Dream* for the thin surface trivia of the next 175 lines: light and
airy, the Intermezzo offers most banal chatter from Goethe's day,
unfamiliar to us and not very interesting to him. *Dream* would, on
the other hand, strike us as a very appropriate designation for the
preceding 386 lines:

"Walpurgis Night" itself. The imagery there held for Faust and
for us the fascination of ancient urges imbedded deep in our personality and revealed to our waking mind only in occasionally recol-

lected snatches of our dreams. The very first lines of "Walpurgis Night" certainly appear to be an introduction to the dream world, especially if we heed the various expressions there which Freudian psychology interprets as sexual symbols (*Knotenstock*—"Knotty stick"; *Labyrinth der Täler*—"labyrinth of valleys"; *diesen Felsen zu ersteigen*—"to mount this rock," etc.).

Why then does Mephistopheles evince such a negative attitude at first? (3837, 3848) He suggested coming here; we have known him to take lascivious pleasure vicariously before. As go-between for Faust and Gretchen:

3543   Hab ich doch meine Freude dran!

    I have my pleasure in it too!

When the cold intellectual looked on their love—or, as he might put it, the sex act—he could only observe that it was a ridiculous, swinish thing to do, and assume that it fulfilled his prophecy:

334   Staub soll er fressen, und mit Lust.

    Dust shall he eat, and with zest.

Mephistopheles' attitude toward the Walpurgis Eve is probably similar. He wants to attend the rites, where witches and warlocks appear to be debasing their humanity. Here he might hope for similar behavior from Faust, who also has a vulnerable libido. Yet even libidinousness in man has certain facets which escape Mephisto. His negative attitude betrays resentment of responses on Faust's part which he cannot quite fathom.

He senses, for example, nothing of the deep fascination that immediately seizes the human wanderer:

3838   FAUST.   Solang ich mich noch frisch auf meinen Beinen fühle,
    Genügt mir dieser Knotenstock.
    Was hilfts, daß man den Weg verkürzt!
    Im Labyrinth der Täler hinzuschleichen,
    Dann diesen Felsen zu ersteigen,
    Von dem der Quell sich ewig sprudelnd stürzt,

Das ist die Lust, die solche Pfade würzt!
Der Frühling webt schon in den Birken,
Und selbst die Fichte fühlt ihn schon;
Sollt er nicht auch auf unsre Glieder wirken?

MEPHISTOPHELES.   Fürwahr, ich spüre nichts davon!
Mir ist es winterlich im Leibe.

FAUST.   So long as in my legs I feel the fresh existence,
This knotted staff suffices me.
What need to shorten so the way?
Along this labyrinth of vales to wander,
Then climb the rocky ramparts yonder,
Wherefrom the fountain flings eternal spray,
Is such delight, my steps would fain delay.
The spring-time stirs within the fragrant birches,
And even the fir-tree feels it now:
Should then our limbs escape its gentle searches?

MEPHISTOPHELES.   I notice no such thing, I vow!
'T is winter still within my body.

Faust is experiencing again grateful sympathy with Nature as he expressed it in the early lines of "Forest and Cavern." He feels in his own members the same surge of life as rises in the birch trees. It is striking how wonderfully at home he feels in these labyrinthine paths. He likes it here. It is more than comfortable; it is fascinating, appetizing (3844). Although probing about in the darkness with a knotty stick may be well enough for man, Mephistopheles demands not only illumination but a direct route as well. His charge to the Will-O'-The-Wisp explicitly associates pleasurable random wandering with human beings:

3863   Ei! ei! Er denkts den Menschen nachzuahmen.
         Geh Er nur grad, ins Teufels Namen!

         Indeed? he'd like mankind to imitate!
         Now, in the Devil's name, go straight.

In order now fully to immerse us in a world of dream, an operatic trio sings, in matter-of-fact unreality, a description of their surroundings. It begins:

3871   In die Traum- und Zaubersphäre
        Sind wir, scheint es, eingegangen.

        We, it seems, have entered newly
        In the sphere of dreams enchanted.

First we pass through desolate space (3875). Despite the grotesque aspect of natural surroundings, they awaken personal memories:

3881   Durch die Steine, durch den Rasen
        Eilet Bach und Bächlein nieder.
        Hör ich Rauschen? hör ich Lieder?
        Hör ich holde Liebesklage,
        Stimmen jener Himmelstage?
        Was wir hoffen, was wir lieben!
        Und das Echo, wie die Sage
        Alter Zeiten, hallet wider.

        O'er the stones, the grasses flowing
        Stream and streamlet seek the hollow.
        Hear I noises? songs that follow?
        Hear I tender love-petitions?
        Voices of those heavenly visions?
        Sounds of hope, of love undying!
        And the echoes, like traditions
        Of old days, come faint and hollow.

Here dwell the most remarkable products of fancy (3893 f.), drawn perhaps from Hieronymus Bosch (whom Goethe's mother called *der Höllen-Bosch*). It is not at all clear whether we are moving past them, or they past us (3906 f.). The trio is introducing us into the world of dream and enchantment, all right, but it is by no means an exotic world: Faust finds it intimately familiar. Going there is an exquisitely pleasurable experience, involving stimuli which reach far down into early strata of personality.

A characteristic of our dreams is the tendency of objects in them to *mean* various things—to use a word of the psychologists and literary critics, they "symbolize" something or other. The interesting thing about these dream objects is of course that they themselves hold more fascination for us than whatever it might be that they stand for. A stunning example of this quality is the dream apparition of gold (3916 ff.).

The lyric which opens "Forest and Cavern" began with an expression of thanks for knowledge of Nature and concluded in reflections on Faust's own personality. The transition from the one subject to the other was a storm:

3228   Und wenn der Sturm im Walde braust und knarrt,
       Die Riesenfichte, stürzend, Nachbaräste
       Und Nachbarstämme quetschend niederstreift
       Und ihrem Fall dumpf-hohl der Hügel donnert,
       Dann führst du mich zur sichern Höhle, zeigst
       Mich dann mir selbst, und meiner eignen Brust
       Geheime, tiefe Wunder öffnen sich.

       And when the storm in forests roars and grinds,
       The giant firs, in falling, neighbor boughs
       And neighbor trunks with crushing weight bear down,
       And falling, fill the hills with hollow thunders,
       Then to the cave secure thou leadest me,
       Then show'st me mine own self, and in my breast
       The deep, mysterious miracles unfold.

Somehow, the storm association was perceived as necessary to the inner logic of the lyric as nexus between grateful contemplation of the outer world and gazing on the secret miracles of the inner self. Those of us who have, perhaps as children, watched the coming and passing of storms in great fascination may be tempted to pause, asking why this should be so: here I shall be content merely to note that the organization of the lyric *is* so, and that again now, in the dramatic progress of "Walpurgis Night," a storm becomes essential to the same kind of subjective transition—a turn to deep introspection.

Mephistopheles' description of a tornado (3938 ff.) may strike us as more impressive than the earlier storm (he is observing it, not recalling it), but the perception is fundamentally the same:

945 Girren und Brechen der Äste!
 Der Stämme mächtiges Dröhnen!
 Der Wurzeln Knarren und Gähnen!
 Im fürchterlich-verworrenen Falle
 Übereinander krachen sie alle,
 Und durch die übertrümmerten Klüfte
 Zischen und heulen die Lüfte.

 Boughs are groaning and breaking,
 The tree-trunks terribly thunder,
 The roots are twisting asunder!
 In frightfully intricate crashing
 Each on the other is dashing,
 And over the wreck-strewn gorges
 The tempest whistles and surges!

As before, the natural calamity alters our frame of mind radically:

954 Ja, den ganzen Berg entlang
 Strömt ein wütender Zaubergesang!

 Yes, the mountain's side along,
 Sweeps an infuriate glamouring song!

This ends the introduction to "Walpurgis Night." We are there, among the "secret wonders of our own breast."

In the next 119 lines Faust is surrounded by indiscriminate groups of figures until he retreats (as in the "Forest and Cavern" lyric) to a secure refuge. This middle section begins in galloping *Knittelvers* and with filthy language, e.g., 3961. What is probably the earliest manuscript evidence of "Walpurgis Night" contains much stronger and more extensive sexuality. It also reveals an interesting connection between the filthy and the obscene. Beside the lines

 Die Ziegen sie riechen
 Die Böcke: sie stincken

The she-goats smell
The he-goats stink

are penciled the verbs *wincken, fechten,* which might yield:

The she-goats beckon
The he-goats prick

Imagery of the final version is certainly no less stark:

3976   Die Gabel sticht, der Besen kratzt,
        Das Kind erstickt, die Mutter platzt.

        The broom it scratches, the fork it thrusts,
        The child is stifled, the mother bursts.

Sometimes it is strikingly beautiful:

3990   Es schweigt der Wind, es flieht der Stern,
        Der trübe Mond verbirgt sich gern.
        Im Sausen sprüht das Zauberchor
        Viel tausend Feuerfunken hervor.

        The wind is hushed, the star shoots by,
        The dreary moon forsakes the sky;
        The magic notes, like spark on spark,
        Drizzle, whistling through the dark.

It is important that all voices are anonymous: our fancy can generalize the personality traits which they bespeak:

3987   STIMMEN (von unten).
                Wir möchten gerne mit in die Höh.
                Wir waschen, und blank sind wir ganz und gar,
                Aber auch ewig unfruchtbar
                . . . .

        STIMME (von oben).
                Wer ruft da aus der Felsenspalte?

STIMME (unten).
>Nehmt mich mit! nehmt mich mit!
>Ich steige schon dreihundert Jahr
>Und kann den Gipfel nicht erreichen.
>Ich wäre gern bei meinesgleichen.

BEIDE CHÖRE.
>Es trägt der Besen, trägt der Stock,
>Die Gabel trägt, es trägt der Bock;
>Wer heute sich nicht heben kann,
>Ist ewig ein verlorner Mann!

HALBHEXE (unten).
>Ich tripple nach so lange Zeit;
>Wie sind die andern schon so weit!
>Ich hab zu Hause keine Ruh
>Und komme hier doch nicht dazu.

CHOR DER HEXEN.
>Die Salbe gibt den Hexen Mut,
>Ein Lumpen ist zum Segel gut,
>Ein gutes Schiff ist jeder Trog:
>Der flieget nie, der heut nicht flog!

VOICE (from below).
>Aloft we'd fain ourselves betake
>We've washed, and are bright as ever you will,
>Yet we're eternally sterile still.
>. . . .

VOICE (from above).
>Who calls from the rocky cleft below there?

VOICE (below).
>Take me, too! take me, too!
>I'm climbing now three hundred years,
>And yet the summit cannot see:
>Among my equals I would be.

BOTH CHORUSES.
  Bears the broom and bears the stock,
  Bears the fork and bears the buck:
  Who cannot raise himself to-night
  Is evermore a ruined wight.

HALF-WITCH (Below).
  So long I stumble, ill bestead,
  And the others are now so far ahead!
  At home I've neither rest nor cheer,
  And yet I cannot gain them here.

CHORUS OF WITCHES.
  To cheer the witch will salve avail;
  A rag will answer for a sail;
  Each trough a goodly ship supplies;
  He ne'er will fly, who now not flies.

These are not aspects of Faust's personality. The eternally sterile seekers after fertility, a man unable to rise, the demi-witch unsatisfied at home, and even here at the Witch's Sabbath are all types known to us, known perhaps better to Goethe in his day (when psychotics were not subject to our many forms of institutionalization)—and presumably known to Faust as well. We find ourselves among a congeries of entelechies crowding one another like bubbles in beer. Mephistopheles is amused (4016 ff.), but Faust is unable to remain detached. He is about to be drawn into the center of the maelstrom when his guardian pulls him back. They retire to a "little space" (4055), although Faust has made his preference clear:

4037   Doch droben möcht ich lieber sein!
       Schon seh ich Glut und Wirbelrauch.
       Dort strömt die Menge zu dem Bösen;
       Da muß sich manches Rätsel lösen.

       Better the summit, I must own:
       There fire and whirling smoke I see.
       They seek the Evil One in wild confusion:
       Many enigmas there might find solution.

The endless source of fascination in our dreams is a promised access
to the forbidden, where "many a puzzle" will surely be solved. The
fascination is so powerful precisely because the promise held out is
never fully granted us. We place the blame on our conscious intellect, personified here in surveillant Mephistopheles.

The third section of "Walpurgis Night" begins harmlessly enough
with those old gentlemen who have been defeated by time (4076 ff.).
Mephisto makes fun of them and of the Huckster-Witch, too, who
is offering what he claims are outmoded tools for vengeance—
Freudians will perceive in poison, jewelry, sword, etc. dream symbolism again. The individuals so far are of a trivial sort, but they *are*
individuals, and this is a new feature in the composition. Awareness
of specific figures permits now the sudden turn toward deepened
psychic significance:

118   FAUST. Wer ist denn das?

       MEPHISTOPHELES.   Betrachte sie genau!
       Lilith ist das.

       FAUST. Wer?

       MEPHISTOPHELES.   Adams erste Frau.

       FAUST. But who is that?

       MEPHISTOPHELES.   Note her especially,
       'T is Lilith.

       FAUST Who?

       MEPHISTOPHELES.   Adam's first wife is she.

It is woman, source of anxiety to man who fears being entrammeled.

120   Nimm dich in acht vor ihren schönen Haaren,
       Vor diesem Schmuck, mit dem sie einzig prangt!
       Wenn sie damit den jungen Mann erlangt,
       So läßt sie ihn so bald nicht wieder fahren.

Beware the lure within her lovely tresses,
The splendid sole adornment of her hair!
When she succeeds therewith a youth to snare,
Not soon again she frees him from her jesses.

Thus an ancient fear serves as fleeting transition to the general theme *woman*. Now Faust's attention is drawn right down to sexual desire. While he and a pretty witch dance, they discuss her jouncing breasts frankly but yet—in that reference (apples) is archly veiled—lasciviously. Now come direct remarks about primary sexual characteristics of old Mephistopheles and the ugly witch. Pleasurable obscenity is realized by means of grotesque exaggeration on subjects which propriety forbids be mentioned under any circumstances.

It is from Goethe himself that certain deletions stem. I may therefore be doing wrong by supplying them:

4138   ein ungeheures Loch (a monstrous hole)

4142   einen rechten Pfropf   (a good stopper)

4143   das große Loch   (the big hole)

Perhaps he hoped that the blank spaces in the text would encourage a reader to imagine greater obscenities in the mouths of the lewd couple—perhaps words even worse than any known to the reader.

A compositional principle of this dream is that ever and anon quite trivial matters pass across the surface of a placid mind, momentarily obscuring its depths, as when the old gentlemen step forward (4076 ff.) or when a nonbeliever—called in Greek a "butt visionary"—denies the forthright sexuality of the dance. What makes such figures trivial is that their obscure temporality contrasts so starkly with the timeless images arising from the depths of Faust's unconscious. Friedrich Nicolai (Berlin publisher, 1733–1811) was already a figure from the past when these lines which allude to him were first published in 1808. While we were listening to him we missed something horrifying:

4178   Ach, mitten im Gesange sprang
        Ein rotes Mäuschen ihr aus dem Munde!

> Ah! in the midst of it there sprang
> A red mouse from her mouth!

Mephistopheles knows how to make the event really disgusting (4180 ff.). In this particular unconscious, *woman* is clearly an ambivalent theme. She is Lilith who ensnares you in her beautiful hair; she is the attractive young witch who arouses you (4132 ff.) then sickens you (4178 f.); she is something more of which we do not learn (4183), for—this insight intrudes itself at last—she is that dearly beloved one whom your drives have destroyed:

195   Fürwahr, es sind die Augen eines Toten,
       Die eine liebende Hand nicht schloß!
       Das ist die Brust, die Gretchen mir geboten,
       Das ist der süße Leib, den ich genoß!

       Forsooth, the eyes they are of one whom, dying,
       No hand with loving pressure closed;
       That is the breast whereon I once was lying,
       The body sweet, beside which I reposed!

The intellect, surprised by the ununderstood power of this vision, denies all by claiming that it is not related to our life at all, but to literature (4194). Mephistopheles is wrong of course. It is of the nature of dreams that they reveal to us truths which we will not admit by day. On account of their fundamental insights, dreams have since time out of mind served as vehicles of prophecy—as does this one in disclosing Gretchen's impending execution. It is a rude awakening for Faust.

The dream has become too much for him, as we recognize when Mephistopheles, unsuccessful in denying the validity of its images, casts about for distractions (4210 ff.). Faust does not awaken right away. The mind emerging from sleep passes first through the day-to-day surface trivia of "Walpurgis Night Dream." The generalized unconscious of "Walpurgis Night" with its universal symbolism is forsaken in favor of the specific material in some particular mind. This contrast between surface consciousness, different in each individual, and the great common property of the deep unconscious is fundamental to composition at this juncture. The specific mind used

for "Walpurgis Night Dream" had to be Goethe's own; the distinc-
tive feature of these 175 lines is that they had only trivial meaning
for him, and have almost none for others. In so far as they still
awaken associations, these are different in each of us—and that is as
it should be.

The Faustian psychic levels discovered by "Walpurgis Night"
may be more complex than those recognized by individual professional psychologists, but I do not wish to undertake detailed analysis
in this sense. It is true that some of the concepts shared by various
schools of psychology in our century invite application in this portion of *Faust*. That is not surprising, because "Walpurgis Night" is
an exploration of the inner depths of personality.

IX

ANTECEDENTS OF PERSONALITY

CLASSICAL WALPURGIS NIGHT

That the first impression is one of great difficulty is partly attributable to Goethe's compositional techniques, but falls mainly to the account of the copious notes to editions in which most people—and, I suppose, all students—encounter the text. Lacking a very clear plot, "Classical Walpurgis Night" relies all the more heavily on a continuity of associations in the reader's mind. Whenever we refer to notes our relationship with the text is broken off and Goethe's basic compositional technique thwarted. There is really nothing much to be gained from them, as a second reading of "Classical Walpurgis Night" will commonly prove: one must refer to the notes again as before, yet may still retain little of the information which an editor was so eager to supply.

But are not the notes essential? How many of the following are known to the average, educated reader? Erichtho, Chiron, Manto, Seismos, Dactyls, Ibycus, Empuse, Oread, Dryad, Phorkyad, Nereus, Cabiri, Telchines, Psylli, Marsi, Dorides, etc. What motive could Goethe have had for using such unfamiliar names, and so many of them? He appears to have taken pains to avoid well-known mythological figures, like Neptune or Venus, in favor of obscure ones like Nereus and Galatea. Why?—No doubt, in order to make an annotated edition necessary.

What would our reaction be if we had no notes? We might, of course, utterly confused, cast the book aside and call *Faust II* impossible. This is precisely what most readers did during the years immediately after Goethe's death. It became fashionable to call *Faust I*

a great work of literature, but *Faust II* mainly senile meanderings.
In our time it has become more fashionable to appreciate *Faust II*
than *Faust I*. Therefore, we read diligently not only the text itself
but the notes to it and the books about it.

Suppose we had no notes, but still did not lay the book aside—
what might our reaction then be to this mass of mythological stran-
gers? We do not know who they are, can only guess at what they
represent. We must read attentively, conjecturally and with an
open mind, trying to glean and infer as much as we can about them
and what each might mean for the whole poem. It may be that we
shall not command the patience to read so slowly and reflectively
through the entire "Classical Walpurgis Night." In that case we shall
read hastily through, but still gain an impression of silhouette, at
least, and general internal organization. Either way, we are probably behaving as the poet hoped we might.

Although editors have chosen to use various divisions and head-
ings for this material, Goethe may have envisioned four main
"scenes":

(1) Pharsalische Felder	"Pharsalian Fields" (7005 ff.)
(2) Peneios	"Peneus River" (7249 ff.)
(3) Am obern Peneios wie zuvor	"At the Upper Peneus" (7495 ff.)
(4) Felsbuchten des Ägäischen Meers	"Rocky Coves of the Aegean Sea" (8034 ff.)

(1) The first of these brings the three travellers to the ancient Phar-
salian battlefields and is then devoted to Mephistopheles' first attempt to come to terms with this alien environment. The Sphinx
asks him: "Just what is to become of you?" (7229) and she is exactly
right: he is going to have to adapt himself by undergoing a radical
metamorphosis here. (2) "Peneus River" deals with Faust's inquiry
after Helen, his ride on Chiron and meeting with Manto. We do not
see him again until the middle of Act III. (3) The next section is just
about as long as the first two put together. Everything begins with

the rise of Seismos pushing up a mountain. The riches in it attract successive waves of settlement; rudimentary political arrangements include involuntary servitude. War impends, breaks out at last, but natural violence destroys what had its origin in violence. Mephistopheles turns up, now lusting after the Lamiae. When Homunculus enters, our attention is diverted briefly to him and the two philosophers debating the origin of things. At the end Mephistopheles transforms himself into a hideous Phorkyad, and we do not see him again until Act III. (4) "Rocky Coves of the Aegean Sea" begins and ends in a giant water spectacle. About forty lines in the middle are also an operatic scene on the water. In the two intervals between water pageants, Thales brings Homunculus first to cross old Nereus, then to silly Proteus for advice on how to originate. Homunculus at last dashes his glass phial to pieces at the love festival where Nereus presides (Nereus thus turns out to be helpful after all). The finale becomes a glorious hymn to love and feminine beauty personified by Galatea. Homunculus' act of immolation allows us to perceive in Galatea a fundamental life force.

The Nature poem which opens "Forest and Cavern" prefigures not only "Walpurgis Night":

228   Und wenn der Sturm im Walde braust und knarrt,
    Die Riesenfichte, stürzend, Nachbaräste
    Und Nachbarstämme quetschend niederstreift
    Und ihrem Fall dumpf-hohl der Hügel donnert,
    Dann führst du mich zur sichern Höhle, zeigst
    Mich dann mir selbst, und meiner eignen Brust
    Geheime, tiefe Wunder öffnen sich.

    And when the storm in forests roars and grinds,
    The giant firs, in falling, neighbor boughs
    And neighbor trunks with crushing weight bear down,
    And falling, fill the hills with hollow thunders,
    Then to the cave secure thou leadest me,
    Then show'st me mine own self, and in my breast
    The deep, mysterious miracles unfold.

but "Classical Walpurgis Night" as well:

3235   Und steigt vor meinem Blick der reine Mond
        Besänftigend herüber, schweben mir
        Von Felsenwänden, aus dem feuchten Busch
        Der Vorwelt silberne Gestalten auf
        Und lindern der Betrachtung strenge Lust.

        And when the perfect moon before my gaze
        Comes up with soothing light, around me float
        From every precipice and thicket damp
        The silvery phantoms of the ages past,
        And temper the austere delight of thought.

"Silvery phantoms of the ages past" seems to be an accurate designation for the figures Faust encounters here, and contemplating them
does have a soothing (*lindern*) effect, the rehabilitation which
Homunculus foresaw (6937 ff.). As in the first Walpurgis Night,
Mephistopheles' initial response is negative, while Faust finds the
surroundings comfortable and familiar (7181 ff.). With characteristic
lack of understanding for mankind, Mephistopheles accounts for
Faust's knowledge of these classical figures by recalling his years as a
frustrated professor to whom they were, he remarks, less attractive
than they now seem to the seeker after Helen (7191 ff.). Faust does
not deign to reply. He may seem to confirm Mephistopheles' conjecture when he immediately inquires about Helen (7196), but
probably neither his academic background nor his present quest is
directly related to those magnificent lines:

7189   Vom frischen Geiste fühl ich mich durchdrungen:
        Gestalten groß, groß die Erinnerungen.

        Fresh spirit fills me, face to face with these—
        Grand are the Forms, and grand the Memories!

He is not referring to his individual past at all, but to cultural
memory. His sense of refreshment derives from recognition of figures out of the great collective conscious of his civilization, enduring
forms which stand above tumult and change:

7245   Sitzen vor den Pyramiden
Zu der Völker Hochgericht,
Überschwemmung, Krieg und Frieden—
Und verziehen kein Gesicht.

We sit before the Pyramids
For the judgment of the Races,
Inundation, War, and Peace—
With eternal changeless faces.

Faust understands that such ancient patterns have their real existence in the conscious of the individual beneficiary of the
Western—in this case Graeco-Roman—tradition, and he correctly
refers to them (according to Aristotelian theory of vision) as pro-
jections of his own eye:

7271   O laßt sie walten,
Die unvergleichlichen Gestalten,
Wie sie dorthin mein Auge schickt!
So wunderbar bin ich durchdrungen!
Sinds Träume? sinds Erinnerungen?
Schon einmal warst du so beglückt.

Let them delay me,
The incomparable Forms!—and sway me,
As yonder to my sight confessed!
How strangely am I moved, how nearly!
Are they but dreams? or memories, merely?
Already once was I so blest.

It would probably be wrong for us to relate the specific "memory" or
"dream" (of the swan approaching Leda and her maidens) merely to
Faust's vision of Leda in "Laboratory" (6903 ff.). A fundamental
point in "Classical Walpurgis Night" is that these are not reflexes of
events in any particular life, but strands of a cultural heritage, the
contemplation of which can rehabilitate an individual in his capacity
as member of a great civilized family.

It seems probable that the major events in "Classical Walpurgis

Night" are roughly synchronous and that none of the three main figures needs be assumed to undergo experiences other than those revealed to us. At the outset each resolves to go his own way (7063 ff.), so that Faust and Homunculus leave Mephistopheles alone to converse with the Griffons, Sphinxes, et al. (7080 ff.) Faust reenters, but exits again shortly (7180-7213). Apparently we should assume that Mephistopheles is continuing his discussion while Faust (7249 ff.) listens to the song of the Sirens and enters into his subsequent adventures. The scene "At the Upper Peneus" (7495 ff.) opens with the Sirens singing *wie zuvor*—"as before"—thus referring us to approximately the same point in time as when Faust is mounting Chiron. The Sirens are dispersed (7501 ff.) by the disruption which Seismos causes. We meet the Griffons and Sphinxes now separated from Mephistopheles, but his further adventures (7676 ff.) "in the plain" must follow almost immediately upon his conversation with them, for he observes (7687 ff.) that it was Seismos who interrupted it (see diagram).

After he has vainly pursued the Lamiae he exchanges a few words with Homunculus (7830 ff.), whose subsequent stroll with the philosophers (7851 ff.) is probably simultaneous with Mephistopheles' bargain with the Phorkyads (7951 ff.). How long it takes them to consummate their agreement none can tell. How long does Faust ride on Chiron's back? What is the duration of the Aegean water festival ("The moon delaying in the Zenith")? Time as sequence has been suspended, so that we are encouraged to assume that Mephistopheles becomes Phorkyas while Faust is in Hades. Perhaps the experiences of both culminate at the instant when Homunculus dashes his glass, begins his development, and time is reinstated.

A major function of Erichtho's speech is to alert us to time overlaps (see especially 7025 ff.). Toward the end of the scene which she opens, the Sphinxes give their really shocking answer to Faust's inquiry about Helen:

7197   Wir reichen nicht hinauf zu ihren Tagen,
        Die letztesten hat Herkules erschlagen.

        We don't reach up to her day;
        Hercules slew the last of us.

ARRIVAL AND FIRST ORIENTATION

7040–7248

Faust drifts away, returns, disappears. Homunculus remains in conversation with Sphinxes, Griffons, etc.

SYNCHRONOUS SCENES ON THE PENEUS RIVER

7249–7494	7495–7675	7676–7850	7830–7950	7951–8034
Faust appears at the Peneus, soon rides away on Chiron, who eventually takes him to Manto and the gates of Hades. Presumably he is in Hades during the scene "Rocky Coves of the Aegean Sea."	Peneus "as before." The rise of Seismos, the emergence of primitive culture sequences occur at the same riverside which Faust left, at the same time as his ride on Chiron and Mephistopheles' pursuit of the Lamiae.	Mephistopheles on the plain complains about the emerging volcanic mountain, pursues the Lamiae, encounters Homunculus.	Homunculus strolls off with Anaxagoras and Thales, who discuss the ongoing events near the Peneus. While Mephistopheles is with the Phorkyads, Homunculus is entering "Coves of the Aegean Sea."	On the other side of the volcanic mountain from where Homunculus is beginning his stroll with his philosophers, Mephistopheles meets the Phorkyads. His transformation into one of them occurs just at the point where time is suspended for Faust and Homunculus.

In Goethe's era it was probably more radical than in ours for an author to ask that time be accepted as a dimension: the Sphinxes dwell too deep in it to have been acquainted with Helen. Chiron lived up at her level—he is the one to talk to:

7200   Der sprengt herum in dieser Geisternacht.

He gallops round throughout this ghostly night,

The Sphinxes see Chiron occasionally: in this "ghostly night," time and space are not discrete categories at all. By coming to the right place, Faust has attained a bygone time. Now if he can but find Chiron, he can go galloping around from one era to another.

Chiron is unable to bring Faust to Helen. She was, after all, only mortal—unlike the other figures encountered so far. Nevertheless, and although Chiron considers Faust's quest a crazy one, he concedes that the usual time measures do not really apply to her, either:

7430   Nie wird sie mündig, wird nicht alt,
        Stets appetitlicher Gestalt,
        Wird jung entführt, im Alter noch umfreit;
        Gnug, den Poeten bindet keine Zeit.

        She grows not old, stays ever young and warm,
        And of the most enticing form;
        Seduced in youth, in age enamoring still,
        Enough! no time can bind the Poet's will.

An obvious effect of remarks like these is finally to "blow our minds," to convince us that our accustomed categories of thought are not obligatory, and thus to prepare us for a freer way of thinking. Chiron transports Faust to Manto, who says:

7481   Ich harre, mich umkreist die Zeit.

        I wait, and Time around me wheels.

Manto is remarkably sanguine about Faust's prospects. The quest for the beloved in the underworld is an archetype which has been realized before—why not again? Orpheus was the individual on the last occasion, but there were others before him and there may be more to come. The archetype, like Manto, says: "I wait, and Time around me wheels."

We are wont to derive our time measurements from oscillations. We designate accumulations of these as shorter or longer intervals. Such objective description has little to do with the way we *experience* time. Time experience occurs primarily in relationship to the growth and decay of structures, especially of organic and social structures. Time as dimension of growth, what Goethe liked to call *werden*, is a major topic of "Classical Walpurgis Night." "At the Upper Peneus" treats it in a most startling way.

The subject under consideration here is the origin of structures. We begin with a mythology of emerging geological forms and of primitive social organization. The scene concludes in Mephistopheles' encounter and eventual union with those hideous daughters of primeval darkness, the Phorkyads. Here he has his major role in "Classical Walpurgis Night," much as Faust dominates the foregoing section, Homunculus the one following. He is, after all, the member of the trio who identifies himself with chaos:

26   Da steh ich schon,
        Des Chaos vielgeliebter Sohn!

                    Me behold,
        The much-beloved son of Chaos old!

These are not abstract words (as 1384): they describe a metamorphosis which has just occurred before our very eyes. "At the Upper Peneus" displays retrograde development from the most rudimentary structures in the physical and social realms, back to pristine formlessness.

In this way an appropriate context has been framed for Homunculus to initiate his earnest efforts to "originate." He comes upon the philosophers Thales and Anaxagoras in a perennial dispute: is the origin of things to be perceived in sudden violence or in gradual accretion? Circumstances observed "At the Upper Peneus" might be adduced to confirm the contentions on either side: Anaxagoras is obviously right as concerns the geological formations, but violence is

destructive of rather than contributory to organic and social structures. Homunculus does well to follow the gentle advocate of
gradualism down to the formless sea.

How is all this related to Faust's quest for Helen? She too must
originate; her shade must acquire form. Mephistopheles' pursuit of
Southern and Northern sluts (Lamiae and the Empuse) has a place
at the beginning of this long scene, as does his representation of
primeval, grandiose feminine ugliness at its close. Faust's longing
for Helen exemplifies man's drive to create form out of flux. Attraction toward the ideally smooth symmetry and clear outlines of the
most beautiful embodiment of femininity implies and no doubt even
arises from that cruder urge toward Helen's unrevealed, unlovely
primary sexual characteristics (symbolized here, as in the first Walpurgis Night, by Mephistopheles' adventures). Homunculus stresses
the question how to originate; Mephistopheles as Phorkyas beckons
us into the womb of chaos.

To open "Rocky Coves of the Aegean Sea," the Sirens turn up for
a third time. Again they play their classical role, enticing us back to
the sea by the atavistic fascination which it holds for all life. The pull
to destruction of self in the ocean is attraction back into the early
womb whence we all arose. If we have indeed been seduced by the
Sirens, then we shall not find ourselves in disagreement with
grumpy old Nereus when he condemns man for being "always the
same" (8094 ff.). We heard his thesis stated for the first time by the
Comic Character in a quite different context:

182   Wer fertig ist, dem ist nichts recht zu machen,
        Ein Werdender wird immer dankbar sein.

        A mind, once formed, is never suited after;
        One yet in growth will ever grateful be.

That was a clear preference for developing beings as distinct from
finished individuals. Nereus objects to mankind because they have
attained to a specific type which does not appear to be evolving
further. He sends Homunculus on to Proteus, advocate of change,
whom he calls a miracle man because he understands origins and
metamorphoses (8152 f.). Proteus has one central piece of advice:

8330   Nur strebe nicht nach höheren Orden:
        Denn bist du erst ein Mensch geworden,
        Dann ist es völlig aus mit dir.

        But struggle not to higher orders!
        Once Man, within the human borders,
        Then all is at an end for thee.

Far be it from Proteus to recommend stability; he admonishes only against striving upward. Unidirectional change is a dead-end street leading eventually to arrested development, as in man. Even Thales' defense of humanity must carry in it the qualifier *zu seiner Zeit*—"It is also a fine thing to be a worthy man *in his day.*" Life in its infinite forms is ever new and different, overflowing precisely that kind of definition in time which confines every individual, even a "worthy man." In post-Darwinian years we naturally assumed that development was by definition "upward," i.e., toward us humans and university professors. One line obviously did lead to us, there is no denying that. Modern genetics tends, however, to take into account the Goethean recognition that there were myriad other possibilities, too. From the point of view of Nereus and Proteus, humanity is by no means a necessary consequence of life, but rather a specified accident out of a limitless potential, and an unfortunate one at that.

    Rejection of man in his rigidity and resistance to change is of fundamental structural importance in "Rocky Coves of the Aegean Sea," a lyrical affirmation of life's infinite creativity and its constantly new forms. Act II culminates in a glorification of love and beauty as the mainsprings of reproductive force. When the Sirens return for a last time, their seduction of us is complete: "All" are willing to deny individuality in a general chorus to the classical four elements in perpetual flux:

8479   SIRENEN: So herrsche denn Eros, der alles begonnen!
                    Heil dem Meere! Heil den Wogen,
                    Von dem heiligen Feuer umzogen!
                    Heil dem Wasser! Heil dem Feuer!
                    Heil dem seltnen Abenteurer!

ALL-ALLE!   Heil den mildgewogenen Lüften!
              Heil geheimnisreichen Grüften!
              Hochgefeiert seid allhier,
              Element ihr alle vier!

SIRENS: Then Eros be ruler, who all things begun!
         Hail, ye Waves! Hail, Sea unbounded,
         By the holy Fire surrounded!
         Water, hail! Hail, Fire, the splendid!
         Hail, Adventure rarely ended!

ALL TOGETHER: Hail, ye Airs that softly flow!
               Hail, ye caves of Earth below!
               Honored now and evermore
               Be the Elemental Four!

It is out of this song to the sea and its praise of colorful fluidity that
Act III arises:

8488   Bewundert viel und viel gescholten, Helena,
       Vom Strande komm ich, wo wir erst gelandet sind,
       Noch immer trunken von des Gewoges regsamem
       Geschaukel.

          Much admired and much reviled, I Helena
       Come from the strand where we have disembarked but now,
       Still giddy from the restless rocking of the waves.

One single, highest *form* emerges out of joyful formlessness. Even if
we must admit humanity to be a dead-end street, we humans are
simply prejudiced in its favor. Hence Galatea, the figure of
anonymous eroticism, is replaced by the clear individuality of Helen.
If her existence can be only for an instant, then glorify the instant
(9417)! The high value of a fleeting moment is a central theme
struck in Act III which then, as we know, takes on its greatest
importance in Act V.

Does "Classical Walpurgis Night" explain how Faust recovers
Helen from antiquity? It might be better to say that it serves as a
transition between that attempt of his in Act I to awaken her and the

brief moment he at last enjoys with her in Act III. Goethe steeps our consciousness in those reflections and colorful images appropriate to the transition. Ostensibly, the process is dramatic: the *dramatis personae:*

Mephistopheles, prurient son of chaos, had his counterparts in the ancient world, for destruction of existing forms is perpetual;

Homunculus earnestly seeks to clothe his essence in life, entering into its fluid, creative abundance;

Faust brings memory, which alone can fix an individual image out of vital flux.

None of these figures ought to be taken as representing or "symbolizing" something. Together they may succeed in awakening in us an appreciation of the realm into which they lead us, that of *Der Vorwelt silberne Gestalten* whence individual personalities draw their specific visage for their instant of survival. One such individual, momentary identity is Helen.

X

IDENTITY

In Chapter IV we approached the Helen Act as an example of the kind of growth *Faust* underwent during Goethe's "classical" period around 1800, language and style, metaphors, metrics and general dramatic form being in purposeful, even ostentatious emulation of the classical Greek. Greek above all are Helen's own attitude and bearing, but especially her manner of identifying herself before us. Establishment of her specific identity, for the sake of which we had to return to classical soil, seemed to be the major function of the first two-hundred lines of Act III.

The question of identity is certainly not restricted to the treatment of Helen, it is a pervasive theme in *Faust*. Both of the Walpurgis Night episodes can be discussed as investigations into components of personality, one as a probe into the depths of an individual psyche, the other as an inquiry about the importance of cultural history. I see the main concern of Act IV and Act V as centering on Faust's desire for continuation of his fleeting moment of individuality. A question basic to the entire Helen Act is: what is the nature of individual identity? Phorkyas forces Helen to ask it, and the deep uncertainty which it arouses in her is shared by us, partly because certain notions fundamental to our own selves are very seriously questioned. One of these arises out of Act II and has been discussed: time understood sequentially.

It is not at all clear that Act III follows Act II in time. Is it not possible that Helen speaks her opening lines while Faust is still talking to Manto, Mephistopheles bickering with the Phorkyads, and Galatea passing before Nereus? Is it not even probable that Mephistopheles, just as soon as he becomes Phorkyas, takes up a position in Menelaus' hall? But what difference does all this really make? Not a sequence of events in time, but a psychologically suitable continuity of impressions on our consciousness leads to Helen's emergence out of the Aegean. Brilliant, colorful water games conclude in a hymn to all elements of Nature, but especially to beauty and love as source of creativity, the production of infinitely changing forms; there emerges one supreme form, the most beautiful of women, capable of arousing desire in old men, Helen. Galatea, lasting epitome of beauty and youth, wanted to tarry for a moment with her father but was drawn on by elemental forces and could not pause; Helen, idealization of precious evanescent identity, lingers. There is a continuity here in Goethe's work on our consciousness, but time sequence is not restored to the poem until the moment when Phorkyas steps out onto the stage of Act III. Her appearance, so unnerving to the Greeks, is a disturbance which effects certain changes—and change implies sequence.

LINES 8697–9126

The initial disturbance is her hideous appearance, to which the girls react in a way that reinforces their identity as we know it already: first in a long-winded recollection of how they witnessed the fall of Troy, then by their ready ability to place Phorkyas in Greek mythology—and, of course, by their silliness:

51   Höre jeglicher Schelte Drohn
     Aus dem verwünschenden Munde der Glücklichen,
     Die von Göttern gebildet sind!

     Hear the threat of every abuse
     From the denouncing mouths of the Fortunate,
     Whom the Gods themselves have fashioned!

Phorkyas replies that modesty and beauty do not go hand in hand— look how she says it! She commences with six long, ambling classical lines:

54   Alt ist das Wort, doch bleibet hoch und wahr der Sinn:
     Daß Scham und Schönheit nie zusammen, Hand in Hand,
     Den Weg verfolgen über der Erde grünen Pfad.

Tief eingewurzelt wohnt in beiden alter Haß,
Daß, wo sie immer irgend auch des Weges sich
Begegnen, jede der Gegnerin den Rücken kehrt.

Old is the saw, and yet its sense is high and true,
That Shame and Beauty ne'er together, hand in hand,
Pursued their way across the green domains of Earth.
Deep-rooted dwells in both such force of ancient hate,
That wheresoever on their way one haps to meet
The other, each upon her rival turns her back.

Such mastery of the Greek style compares more than favorably with Helen's own. Note, for example, Helen's remark that only the mistress is entitled to scold the servants, four highly stylized lines (8784 ff.). This is the classical way, or at least the way of the classical drama: to speak in eternal verities, proceeding from a general truth to a specific adaptation appropriate for the given situation. Phorkyas was not quite through with her remarks about beauty and modesty:

8760   Dann eilet jede wieder heftiger, weiter fort,
        Die Scham betrübt, die Schönheit aber frech gesinnt,
        Bis sie zuletzt des Orkus hohle Nacht umfängt,
        Wenn nicht das Alter sie vorher gebändigt hat.—

        Then forth again vehemently they hasten on,
        Shame deep depressed, but Beauty insolent and bold,
        Till her at last the hollow night of Orcus takes,
        If Age hath not beforehand fully tamed her pride.

Act III begins egregiously Greek. It ceases to be *purely* Greek when a figure towers in buskins poking fun at the classical usages so rigidly adhered to up until now. Since Phorkyas' first lines are a travesty of the style that has gone before, her entrance into Act III skews the stage before us, and the distortion has just begun.

Helen bravely upholds her now threatened character as Greek aristocrat (8784 ff.), but Phorkyas replies to her in heavy sarcasm shockingly inappropriate for addressing royalty:

8796   HELENA.   Hast du das Haus des Königs wohl verwahrt bisher
        Anstatt der Hausfrau, solches dient zum Ruhme dir;

derbe Frauen, gefällig wild
earthy women, pleasingly wanton

From the majolica collection in the Goethe-Haus, Weimar

Doch jetzo kommt sie selber: tritt nun du zurück,
Damit nicht Strafe werde statt verdienten Lohns!

PHORKYAS. Den Hausgenossen drohen bleibt ein großes Recht,
Das gottbeglückten Herrschers hohe Gattin sich
Durch langer Jahre weise Leitung wohl verdient.

HELEN. If thou the Palace hitherto hast guarded well
In place of Mistress, so much to thy credit stands;
But now that she herself hath come, shouldst thou return
Lest punishment, in place of pay deserved, befall!

PHORKYAS. To threaten the domestics is a right assured,
Which she, the spouse august of the God-prospered king,
By many years of wise discretion well hath earned.

The Chorus, outraged, rises to Helen's defense. Stichomythy en-
sues and the exchange takes proverbial form—what could be more
characteristic of classical drama? But the effect becomes uncanny as
we begin to perceive that charges and countercharges are entirely
too apt: the servants' taunts are quite as applicable to Mephistopheles as to Phorkyas; similarly, Mephisto/Phorkyas' insults are
just ambivalent enough to fit ordinary servant girls as well as phantoms long deceased. At last the ambiguity of identities is frankly
admitted (8822 ff.). Helen commands an end to the quarrel on
grounds that it is opening old wounds (8834 ff.)—precisely what
Phorkyas intended. Recalling the past permits Phorkyas to speak
forthrightly of Helen's double identity at an earlier time (8872 f.).
Helen pleads:

8874   Verwirre wüsten Sinnes Aberwitz nicht gar!
      Selbst jetzo, welche denn ich sei, ich weiß es nicht.

      Make wholly not confused my clouded, wandering sense!
      Even in this moment, who I am I cannot tell.

Phorkyas is out to enhance precisely this uncertainty, but the
Chorus again comes to the Queen's defense (8882 ff.). They constitute the formal Greek environment which, intact, contributes to the
stability of Helen's identity (8903 ff.). Phorkyas, by insinuating her-

self among the figures surrounding Helen, both attacks their protective wall and threatens to dissolve the clear citadel of the Queen herself,

8907   Die Gestalt aller Gestalten.

        The Form of all forms.

We would certainly be wrong to regard the figures before us as people: we are in a world of abstracts. Phorkyas is not working on persons; she is displaying for us how an entity can be transmuted. The process may seem more chemical than dramatic.

Phorkyas would demonstrate that classical form cannot be reconciled with acceptable content. She ostensibly accedes to the Chorus' demand that Helen be treated with respect, and she even speaks in a laudatory tone (8909 ff.) but, if *what* she says has at last become appropriate, *how* she says it is not: Phorkyas speaks in modern trochees—and Helen responds in kind! Her classical character wavers, and metrics are giving the lie to the ostensible agreement that Helen and Phorkyas are aristocratic Greek woman and her servant. Phorkyas now says (8917 ff.) in effect: "All right, then, let us be Greeks. What commands does the Queen give her servant? Preparation of a sacrifice? Very well, here is all the paraphernalia which I as competent servant place at the Queen's disposal. The sacrificial animal—this is to be you, is it not, Queen Helen? As for these girls here, they shall be hanged from the rafters later in good Greek style, as we know it from the *Odyssey*." When Phorkyas abates her sarcasm and even returns to classical meter, the *content* of her remarks is that classical times are over and done with:

8930   Gespenster!—Gleich erstarrten Bildern steht ihr da,
        Geschreckt, vom Tag zu scheiden, der euch nicht gehört.

        Ye Phantoms!—like to frozen images ye stand,
        In terror thus from Day to part, which is not yours.

We ourselves feel the full impact of her scorn because Phorkyas, now openly Mephistophelian, includes all mankind in her harsh reproach:

8932   Die Menschen, die Gespenster sämtlich gleich wie ihr,
        Entsagen auch nicht willig hehrem Sonnenschein.

        Men, a race of spectres like you, one and all,
        Renounce not willingly the bright beams of the sun;

Continuing to couch a modern devil's irony in classical meter and
suitable Greek terminology, Phorkyas requires that everything be
readied for the sacrifice—at last the Chorus capitulates.

    Its leader admits that the Greek way, so viciously parodied, does
indeed appear impossible under the circumstances:

8947   Die Königin stehet sinnend an der Seite hier,
        Die Mädchen welken gleich gemähtem Wiesengras.

        The Queen is standing, sunk in thought, beside us here,
        The maidens wither like the late-mown meadow grass;

Although Phorkyas has not yet had her fill of heavy-handed satire,
hence still rambles considerably, Helen cannot help but take some
interest in the foreign, warlike people reported to have settled in
the vicinity during her absence. She asks a question which strikes to
the heart of the matter so far as she is concerned:

9005   Ist Einer Herr?

        Is one man Chief?

That is the strategic consideration; the next question is tactical:

9010   Wie sieht er aus?

        What does he look like?

Phorkyas breaks right into the middle of the metrical line, for the
issue is clearly decided now, and she can throw off all pretense of
being Greek:

Nicht übel.

Not bad.

She finally moves even Helen to a quite un-Greek outburst:

9047   Du fällst
       Ganz aus der Rolle.

              Thou fall'st
       Entirely from thy part.

Helen is right. This is no longer Phorkyas at all, but a Northern
devil in highly idiomatic German, obviously prejudiced in favor of
Rhineland architecture and alert to any opportunity to cut the
Greeks (9012, 9019).

We have observed before this how Mephistopheles chooses to
manipulate people. He prefers to act as mere helper and guide
where possible (2376 f., 3707), and he always insists on full implication of the principal (the Emperor, for example). As he had straight
away told Panthalis he would (8954 ff.), he now demands Helen's
express compliance:

9049   Sagst mit Ernst vernehmlich Ja!

       Say with grave distinctiveness, Yes!

Sometimes a little pressure must be applied before unequivocal
agreement can be exacted:

9054   PHORKYAS.   Hast du vergessen, wie er deinen Deiphobus,
       Des totgekämpften Paris Bruder, unerhört
       Verstümmelte, der starrsinig Witwe dich erstritt
       Und glücklich kebste? Nas und Ohren schnitt er ab
       Und stümmelte mehr so: Greuel war es anzuschaun.

       HELENA.   Das tat er jenem, meinetwegen tat er das.

PHORKYAS. Um jenes willen wird er dir das gleiche tun!

PHORKYAS. Hast thou forgotten how he thy Deiphobus,
Brother of fallen Paris, who with stubborn claim
Took thee, the widow, as his fere, did visit with
Unheard-of mutilation? Nose and ears he cropped,
And otherwise disfigured: 't was a dread to see.

HELEN. That did he unto him: he did it for my sake.

PHORKYAS. Because of him he now will do the like to thee.

As always Mephistopheles, even as Phorkyas, controls the stage
directions if need be—

Trompeten in der Ferne; der Chor fährt zusammen.

Trumpets in the distance; the Chorus starts in terror.

and Helen's consent comes at last (9074). The colors run, as clear
bright classical lines fade behind a pale Romantic fog. Phorkyas has
made her catch and Mephistopheles has persuaded Helen that her
identity is not limited to the stage of classical Greece. The scenes
"Inner Courtyard" and "Arcadia" are now possible, where Helen
will enjoy experiences alien to her earlier selves.

The girls are uncertain (9113 ff.) whether they are tripping along
or being borne through the enveloping fog. It obscures all forms at
first, but out of it at last arise the dark outlines of Faust's castle. This
transition to "Inner Courtyard" is analogous to the scenes enclosing
the entire Act. Before Act III, individual forms had yielded to flow-
ing color while protean, unindividuated life forces were praised;
from the motley conglomerate the lens of Act III caught up for a
moment the classical figures and focused them on a Northern culture. At the end of Act III the Chorus will again sing of the same
four elements praised in that earlier paean. Euphorion, Helen,
Faust, Panthalis, each in his own way, will forego at last the specific
identity established momentarily for "Arcadia."

EUPHORION (9596–9938)

The Euphorion figure explores continuity of personality. Phorkyas introduces him to us as a riddle at whose identity we are
expected to puzzle. She describes him first as a genius without
wings, a fawn (9603). He takes his strength from the earth, so that
we associate him with Antaeus (9604) and are encouraged when we
learn that we have guessed right (9611). Since he is a poetic spirit,
however, he may be Phoebus Apollo (9620). The Chorus assures us
that there are no new identities under the sun (9637 ff.), and they
think that he must really be Hermes of old. Phorkyas/Mephisto is of
course not willing to concede such a point. She argues that important developments have occurred since the Greeks (9679 ff.), and
the beauty of modern poetry (9685 ff.) actually convinces the girls of
this.

Thus we succeed in "solving" the Euphorion puzzle by identifying him with modern poetry. But now we begin to suspect that some
one poet is being alluded to. The features of his personality accumu-
late: he is associated with Greece (9825 f.), with war (9835 ff.), with
revolution (9843 ff.), with struggle to remain free (9855 f.). He is
determined to take up arms (9870 ff.) and looks forward to martial
death (9888 ff.). By this point we obviously have to assume that the
one poetic spirit foremost in the mind that created Euphorion must
be a Romantic poet—yet at the same time, precisely on account of
the many allusions by which we have been playfully led to this
solution, we have to concede that the Romantic is himself only one
variant of a basic *Gestalt* which manifests itself in several mutually
related and even interdependent figures (e.g. Hermes, Phoebus,
Antaeus). The most startling of all the identities accumulating in
Euphorion flashes up in the final moment of his existence: the beloved boy who dares too much, then falls meteorlike to destruction
is, of course, Icarus (9901).

At last stage directions inform us that *we seem to recognize a
well-known figure*. The beautiful elegy, perhaps the finest of all
monuments to Lord Byron, begins with an assurance:

9907   Nicht allein!—wo du auch weilest!
        Denn wir glauben dich zu kennen.

Not alone! where'er thou bidest;
For we know thee what thou art.

Here the personal pronouns can present a real conundrum to anyone who ponders them too long. We are obviously expected to
recognize someone in Euphorion-Icarus. The *we* which technically
refers to the Chorus becomes *we the audience,* or perhaps the author speaking editorially to Euphorion-Byron. But since the poem
to Byron began already in 9907,

Nicht allein!—Wo du auch weilest,

Not alone! where'er thou bidest;

the *thee* whom *we* recognize in Byron (9908) must be something
more: do we recognize someone in Byron? I think "we" the poet
must recognize ourselves there, while "we" the audience perceive
Goethe in Byron, much as we recognized Phoebus Apollo and others in Euphorion:

9937   Denn der Boden zeugt sie wieder,
       Wie von je er sie gezeugt.

       For the soil shall generate them,
       As it hath done heretofore.

The Euphoric identity, like Helen's, is continuous both before and
beyond the instant of any one lifetime. However widely separated in
time or by culture they may be, such figures as Hermes, Byron and
Goethe are precious individual variants on one ideal human potential. Gerhart Hauptmann and Thomas Mann, who sometimes liked
to imagine themselves as Goethe's spirit, must have taken particular
pleasure in 9937 f.

LINES 9939–10038

Phorkyas fixes our attention on the identity question when she
uses a most remarkable turn of speech. Of Helen's garment she says
to Faust: "Hold it fast!"

9952   Es trägt dich über alles Gemeine rasch
        Am Äther hin, solange du dauern kannst.

        'T will bear thee swift from all things mean and low
        To ether high, so long thou canst endure.

What remains of the Helen experience will ennoble Faust's existence as long as he *endures*. We usually say "as long as you live," an
everyday phrase which bespeaks our assumption that when you are
no longer alive, for practical purposes, things are pretty much over.
By using the remarkable expression, "as long as you last," Phorkyas
makes us regard Faust also, like Helen and Euphorion, as an identity which may continue for a span quite apart from that of an
organic lifetime. As a matter of fact, in the present context it would
be pretty silly for her to use an expression like "as long as you live":
we have not been observing living beings at all. They are more vital
than life in that they are charged with more meaning than one life
can have. The figures here mean something in many generations of
individual lives. Helen has certainly lasted longer than her people
lived.

        The recognition that an individual's identity may under some
circumstances last longer than he lives accomplishes a major step in
the development of the central theme in *Faust II*. Act III closes now
in varied illumination of this particular area of inquiry. Helen descends to Hades, and Panthalis follows:

9967   Ihrer Sohle sei
        Unmittlebar getreuer Mägde Schritt gefügt!

             Now, upon the track,
        Let straightway follow her the step of faithful maids!

It is she who insists in ingenuous certainty on the possibility of
"preserving the self":

9981   Wer keinen Namen sich erwarb noch Edles will
        Gehört den Elementen an: so fahret hin!
        Mit meiner Königin zu sein, verlangt mich heiß;
        Nicht nur Verdienst, auch Treue wahrt uns die Person.

Who hath not won a name, and seeks not noble works,
Belongs but to the elements: away then, ye!
My own intense desire is with my Queen to be;
Service and faith secure the individual life.

Most individuals will, according to Panthalis, yield up their personalities in the eternal flux which so appropriately frames Act III.
But any can if not by dint of extraordinary merit then by virtue of
great devotion discover the "Undiscoverables" (9969), as Panthalis
now expects to do by placing her feet carefully into Helen's
footsteps. The girls do not want to go along with her, and they do
not have to. None is compelled to endure beyond his individual life;
one may merely go on living instead. To do so the girls have to
surrender their several identities, of course, but not their share in
that protean life which Act II praised so rapturously. They sing:

985   Zurückgegeben sind wir dem Tageslicht,
       Zwar Personen nicht mehr,
       Das fühlen, das wissen wir,
       Aber zum Hades kehren wir nimmer!
       Ewig lebendige Natur
       Macht auf uns Geister,
       Wir auf sie vollgültigen Anspruch.

       Given again to the daylight are we,
       Persons no more, 't is true,
       We feel it and know it,
       But to Hades return we never!
       Nature, the Ever-living,
       Makes to us spirits
       Validest claim, and we to her also.

As Act II ended in song to the four Aristotelian elements, the
Chorus here also raises a hymn to earth (9992 ff.), air (9999 ff.),
water (10005 ff.) and fire (10011 ff.). The image of the sun-drenched
grape interrelates all four elements as they are subsumed in life.
Bacchus (10017 ff.) permits man in drunken stupors and in the orgy
to perceive his fundamental kinship to elemental forces. This is the
god of the fertility rite, which plunges the individual consciousness
into a collective, orgiastic affirmation of anonymous life.

10034   Nichts geschont! Gespaltne Klauen treten alle Sitte nieder,
         Alle Sinne wirbeln taumlig, gräßlich übertäubt das Ohr.
         Nach der Schale tappen Trunkne, überfüllt sind Kopf und Wänste;
         Sorglich ist noch ein- und andrer, doch vermehrt er die Tumulte:
         Denn um neuen Most zu bergen, leert man rasch den alten
            Schlauch!

         Naught is spared! The cloven hoofs tread down all decent custom;
         All the senses whirl bewildered, fearfully the ear is stunned.
         Drunkards fumble for the goblets, over-full are heads and
            paunches;
         Here and there hath one misgivings, yet increases thus the tumult;
         For, the fresher must to garner, empty they the ancient skin!

The motif of living forms in constant flux arose in Act II. The central
purpose of Act III was to establish clearly and nobly the possibility
of individual identity in the face of flux. The individual enjoys his
bond with life for only an instant, a precious one which he is duty
bound to treasure:

9418   Dasein ist Pflicht, und wärs ein Augenblick.

         Being is duty, though a moment held.

The meeting between Faust and Helen in its touching beauty is
conceived to help us appreciate the value of each unique, present
moment:

9382   FAUST.   Die Gegenwart allein—
         HELENA.   ist unser Glück.

         FAUST.   Our present only
         HELENA.   is happiness.

The moment of individuated life is valuable beyond compare because it will never recur. While amorphous life floods on indefi-
nitely, Helen, Euphorion and Panthalis have shown Faust that individuality might also be, in its own way, enduring.
   What a tremendous range of meaning the *Faust* text demands for
the word *Augenblick*—"moment"! By the end of Act III we have

radically extended our apprehension of the famous lines:

1699   Werd ich zum Augenblicke sagen:
        Verweile doch! du bist so schön,

so that when Faust at the grave uses almost the same words,

1581   Zum Augenblicke dürft ich sagen:
        Verweile doch, du bist so schön!

we understand something entirely different. We might translate freely:

1699   If I shall come to know a single instant in life so gratifying
        that I would like for it to linger . . .

and

1581   (By achieving such a sociopolitical structure as I have
        just described) I would be entitled to expect my precious
        instant of individuality to endure.

Act III with its exploration of identity has been pivotal in accomplishing for *Augenblick*—"moment"—this breadth of meaning.

XI

KNOWLEDGE
AND ACADEME

The question as to the possibility of knowing is raised by Faust's opening monologue, hence at the outset of the play proper. It was probably basic in Goethe's very earliest thinking about *Faust*, so that whatever aspects of the work might come into our consideration, we are never entirely without the awareness of an underlying, persistent question: can man know? That is indeed the essence of the Faust theme from its earliest recorded treatments in the 16th century. There had been many before Doctor Faustus who had entered into compacts with the devil—perhaps the best known at the time was Theophilus, who was said to have signed away his soul in return for high position in the Church. In the very earliest Faust book which we can infer, however, this scholarly hero makes *his* deal with the devil in hope of access to forbidden knowledge. Although the publishing houses of the late 16th and early 17th centuries were prone to spin out the fantastic worldly benefits accruing from the pact, most of these tales had been told about various adventurers prior to Faustus, and few of them became permanently attached to him now. He held enduring fascination for poet and people as the man who would *know*.

What does Faust want to know? Like his understanding of the "moment," his quest for knowledge changes radically as the poem develops. In the famous opening monologue he makes it pretty clear that he has a surfeit of one kind of knowledge:

366   Zwar bin ich gescheiter als alle die Laffen,
       Doktoren, Magister, Schreiber und Pfaffen.

> I'm cleverer, true, than those fops of teachers,
> Doctors and Magisters, Scribes and Preachers;

while in true understanding he not only feels himself wanting, but even cut off from any realistic hope (364). Furthermore, when he tries to express what it is he wants to know, he tends towards words like *erkennen* (382) or *schauen* (384). He avoids the strictly cognitive word *wissen* (371), is sick of it (1749), even contrasts it with the understanding he longs for (1768–71), which comprehends the broadest range of human experiences. By way of emphasizing the irrelevance of mere *wissen*, the young Goethe introduced us to poor Wagner as one who uncritically cherishes data knowledge for its own sake. The Wagner of the Faust Book and of puppet-play tradition was not of this sort at all but merely a collaborator with Faust and his successor in sorcery; Goethe's alteration of Wagner's traditional role reflects his youthful eagerness to ridicule academe.

Ridicule of academe had of course been part and parcel of the Faust theme from the beginning. The very earliest collection of tales of which we have record is one presumed to have been written down by Wolf Wambach, chronicler of Erfurt, a university town. Faust appears before the professors and students in order to conjure up out of the past those Greek heroes and other mythological figures which they are studying about in the abstract. They are aghast at the horrible aspect of the "real" thing, and flee when Cyclops appears with some of Ulysses' men dangling from his teeth. Again, Faust offers to recover some lost Greek manuscripts, thus providing the scholars with the complete works of authors whom they profess to venerate, but they will have none of it: the devil might falsify the record by slipping in blasphemous or otherwise objectionable passages. What is the academic world, after all, other than that segment of society which makes a special claim to *know*—or at least to offer access to knowledge? Faust becomes with Goethe the member of the academic sector who says: "All the stores of academe are worthless." If there is no access to knowledge *here*, where in the world can such access be found? Still, Faust's posture is anything but negative, for he is after all assuming that there is somewhere something truly worth knowing. More important, he shows us that there is at least one man willing to sacrifice himself both in this world and in the next to achieve it. This is the way in which the Faust theme (like all the great conceptions of mankind) postulates something better than man's life on this earth.

A poet who wants to insist on something nobler than what he has found in our sublunary realm is nevertheless compelled to make do with what this earth has to offer in subject matter if he expects to communicate effectively: Christ, for example, while exclusively concerned with eternal life, characteristically resorted to everyday temporal illustrations in his parables. As a consequence of the same paradoxical situation, reform writers, like the Naturalists for instance, have often directed their readers' attention not to the ideals so important to them, but rather to the terrible imperfections in the world as it is. They do not seek to prove positively that their higher truth does exist, but find their most effective argument to lie in trenchant insistence on the inadequacy and inacceptability of the untruths and partial truths accessible to us: "See what a sorry world this is! Man alive can never come to terms with it. I believe in something better—not because it is easy to do so, but because I must." It is in this sense that the academic world comes into the Faust tradition, which submits to us the wise men and the sages, the shoddy which they offer for truth, and asks the rhetorical question: can we accept *this?* Goethe appears to have conceived Wagner as such a representative of academe:

600   Mit Eifer hab ich mich der Studien beflissen:
      Zwar weiß ich viel, doch möcht ich alles wissen.

      Most zealously I seek for erudition:
      Much do I know—but to know all is my ambition.

                              WAGNER

At first he was little more than a foil to Faust (here, lest there be any mistake about it, is the kind of knowledge which Faust is *not* seeking). The maturer Goethe who wrote "Before the City Gates" goes farther. He seems to have acquired a genuine distaste for the professional custodians of knowledge, unlike any known to the younger poet. Wagner here is no longer a superficial parody, but a well considered image of academic man drawn with harsh strokes, feature by despicable feature. Goethe does not waste a line. Wagner likes to associate with what he takes to be his ilk and avoids the common salt of the earth (941 ff.). On the other hand, he thinks it is a fine thing to be admired by these same common folk with whom he would not deign to associate (1011 ff.). The most damning feature which Goethe lends him is a self-protectiveness which wisely measures each task not in terms of its importance, but against one's own competence. *Homo academicus* asks not: where are the utmost limits of my capability?—but rather: what is the most that can reasonably be expected of me?

957   Tut nicht ein braver Mann genug,
       Die Kunst, die man ihm übertrug,
       Gewissenhaft und pünktlich auszuüben?

       A good man does his honest share
       In exercising, with the strictest care,
       The art bequeathed to his possession!

This trait in Wagner is all the more understandable since he is innocent of strong desires (we have his own word for it that he is an enemy of anything coarse). What Faust experiences as an urgent drive is something that his famulus feels as little more than an itch (1100 f.). Besides, Wagner is a coward (1126 ff.), troubled by a philosophy which conceives the whole daemonic realm as conspiring against him in particular (note the pronouns in 1130 ff.). Slave to his physical self, he prefers the comforts of home to the inclement out-of-doors (1142 ff.). Of course, Wagner's awed description of the spirits (1130 ff.) has the important structural function in *Faust* of opening our minds to the imminence of Mephistopheles. Even while Wagner speaks, Faust is contemplating instead with unflinching curiosity precisely that realm of possibility to which the famulus resolutely closes his mind.

Goethe might have let the miserable fellow go his way after line 601, but Wagner was obviously a figure who still interested him when he returned to *Faust* at the end of the century; we probably have Goethe's personal acquaintance with scholars during the 1780s and 1790s to thank for that. His interests in geology, botany, anatomy, and even chemistry led him to seek the advice of academic luminaries on numerous occasions, and his sharp disagreement with their opinion in at least one field, optics, is notorious. Yet this is by no means the first or the only science in which he long and eagerly sought professorial approval for his work in vain.

In 1784, he wrote a charming little treatise on the premaxillary bone which to this day stands out as a milestone paper in the history of science both in its exemplary morphological method and because it effectively refuted the idea that man can be distinguished from other vertebrata on the basis of a simpler upper jawbone structure. Goethe was delighted with his work and had it translated into Latin to assure that the extravagant copies which he personally dispatched to distinguished physiologists in Europe would in fact be read by them. They read them—and rejected Goethe's contentions almost unanimously. At the time when "Before the City Gates" was written (almost a generation later), the premaxilla in man, which Goethe had traced out with his own eye and sketched meticulously with his own pen, was still unrecognized by the experts. Already in the spring of 1785, he had remarked to his old friend Johann Heinrich Merck: "I expect a professional scholar to deny his five senses. They are seldom concerned with the living concept of an inquiry, but only with what has been said about it."

At the high point of the entire *Faust* poem, Faust sings with Helena the famous credo of life and of science:

9382   Die Gegenwart allein ist unser Glück

        Presence is our entire happiness

One of the most delightful burlesques of the scholar is offered by the *Gelahrter*, "perfesser," who, when Helen is presented to his very eyes, fulfills Goethe's scornful words to Merck:

6535   Die Gegenwart verführt ins Übertriebene,
        Ich halte mich vor allem ans Geschriebene.

        Presence leads us to exaggeration,
        I'll stick to the written word.

By outlasting his own era, Goethe in his 70s finally experienced a new generation's acceptance of that fifty-year-old discovery of his, but there had in the meantime arisen other occasions to renew his resentment of the "professional scholar." In *Faust II* Wagner has achieved the adulation (6643 ff.) which we heard him envy "Before the City Gates," but he appears as ridiculous as ever. Goethe still finds him characterized by the monstrous disproportion between dry-as-dust theorizing about the world and the mysterious warmth of Nature which an alien to her can never suspect. This character of the scientist has attained its permanent symbol for movie-goers of our century in Dr. Frankenstein, whose vanity in great knowledge and failure to apprehend the miracle of life leads him to the acme of arrogance, manufacture of a synthetic man. Common folk always take great scientists to be crackpots:

6867   Ein großer Vorsatz scheint im Anfang toll;
      Doch wollen wir des Zufalls künftig lachen,
      Und so ein Hirn, das trefflich denken soll,
      Wird künftig auch ein Denker machen.

      Insane, at first, appears a great intent;
      We yet shall laugh at chance in generation;
      A brain like this, for genuine thinking meant,
      Will henceforth be a thinker's sure creation.

Obviously, Wagner expects to create Homunculus in his own image—but there remain mysteries in life not dreamt of in the philosophy of him who, as it turns out, cannot comprehend what he thought to be his own creature, and certainly cannot control him. As we leave Wagner for the last time it is Homunculus who voices Goethe's bitter mockery of the man who thinks he knows (6988 ff.).

STUDENT

If the early scenes establish any one fact clearly, it is the great seriousness to Faust of his quest for insight. This is why he bargains with Mephistopheles for personal experience in the world: it may not appear to him a very promising avenue, but it is the only one open, and he is sufficiently resolute to try it. All this presupposes of course the utter vanity of academic avenues, which Faust has presumably explored thoroughly before the play opens. After the agreement with Mephistopheles is consummated, however, Goethe still retains one further satire of the faculties so bitterly enumerated by Faust at the outset.

Mephistopheles takes over Wagner's role as advocate of a purely cognitive approach to understanding and, in professor's robes, recommends it to the Student. First of all he praises logic for the admirable clarity with which it explains thought processes—of course you mustn't expect it to teach you *how* to think (1922 ff.). Triumphantly impractical, academic thinking is unrelated to reality. This is why reasonable men are selective about what they study:

1936   Wer will was Lebendigs erkennen und beschreiben,
        Sucht erst den Geist herauszutreiben.

        He who would study organic existence,
        First drives out the soul with rigid persistence.

Once the pupil has become fully "rational" in the sense that he espouses logic as distinct from common sense, he can advance to metaphysics, a realm so wonderfully irrelevant to the world as to permit magnificent abstract performance:

1950   Da seht, daß Ihr tiefsinnig faßt,
        Was in des Menschen Hirn nich paßt!
        Für was drein geht und nicht drein geht,
        Ein prächtig Wort zu Diensten steht.

        See that you most profoundly gain
        What does not suit the human brain!
        A splendid word to serve, you'll find,
        For what goes in—or won't go in—your mind.

Since the matter has no heart, rules and regulations become paramount (1954 ff.). Law is a superior example of academic study, where one never deals with the case at hand, always with what is in the books (1972 ff.).

The overriding importance of words and phrases in the scholar's life is accounted for by the irrelevance of academic study. So long as all academic viewpoints are unrelated to experience, one hypothesis is just as acceptable as another. For this reason, it is advisable that a student hold to a single teacher (1988 f.), lest one abstraction become confused with a second, or even be contradicted by a third. In the absence of external validation, what other basis would one have for distinguishing, much less discriminating among the various doctrines propounded? Only by ignoring reality can *homo academicus* attain to the certainty which marks his species:

91   Dann geht Ihr durch die sichre Pforte
        Zum Tempel der Gewißheit ein.

        Then through the safest gate you'll enter
        The temple-halls of Certainty.

Medicine at last comes off with the most vicious commentary, because the assumption is made that in this field the academician himself recognizes how little he knows—how little anyone can know—and hence decides to draw at least a material profit for his efforts (2012 ff.). Here crass opportunism pays off (2017 f.), thus some points arise which are not entirely academic, like bedside manner (2019 ff.).

BACCALAUREATE

Professor Immanuel Kant at Königsberg may be regarded as the founder of German Idealism. He called explicit and detailed attention to the merely indirect and fallible access of the human mind to objects and ideas outside it. An obvious corollary of Kant's limitation on the potential of reason was the somewhat paradoxical one drawn by Johann Gottlieb Fichte, professor at Jena, who argued that the world which we know must in great measure be the mind's own product, any actual objects (presumably the source of impressions on the subject) being relatively less important. It was in Fichte's terminology that the German pronoun *ich* became so important as a noun. Goethe, in sending a Fichte essay to a friend in 1794, enclosed the following note:

> Only a cordial greeting to accompany the enclosed article. I hope that you, dear non-ego [*Nicht-Ich*], will, when you have a chance, communicate something of your thoughts about it to my ego. Farewell, and say hello to all of the good little non-egos round about you.

Although Goethe here appears only amused at the categorical nature of Fichte's work, he soon discovered the man to be equally opinionated in his day-to-day relationships. At last, in spite of his efforts to smooth over disagreements which arose between Fichte and the authorities, Goethe was unable to prevent the departure of the refractory professor from the Jena faculty.

I do not doubt that it was Fichte and his doctrinaire followers, the more programmatic of the Romanticists, who served as models for the Student when he returns as Baccalaureate:

6687   Doch diesmal ist er von den Neusten:
        Er wird sich grenzenlos erdreusten.

        He is of the school new-founded,
        And his presumption will be quite unbounded.

It is the familiar Fichtean solipsism to which a line like 6791 refers:

        Wenn ich nicht will, so darf kein Teufel sein.

        Save through my will, no Devil can there be.

Goethe deliberately associates this philosophical outlook with youth:

6793   Dies ist der Jugend edelster Beruf:
        Die Welt, sie war nicht, eh ich sie erschuf!

        This is Youth's noblest calling and most fit!
        The world was not, ere I created it;

The young Romanticists lived during the Napoleonic occupation of much of Germany, so that by history's whim they provided the first German patriots in the nationalistic, even jingoistic sense which

Goethe satirizes here:

6771   Im Deutschen lügt man, wenn man höflich ist.

        One lies in German, would one courteous be.

Goethe expressly denied that he had Fichte, his followers, or any such specific group in mind which he introduced the Baccalaureate, and it is indeed clear that he is eager to take his whacks at young people in general (6774 ff.). He allows the Baccalaureate to make only one sane observation: that teachers are not truthful with their pupils (6750 ff.). Otherwise he is a fool. The essential ingredient of his foolishness is the very quality which he presumably learned at the university: absolute reliance on his own intellect and the theories which it evolves independent of empirical checks:

6758   Erfahrungswesen! Schaum und Dust!
        Und mit dem Geist nicht ebenbürtig!

        Experience! mist and froth alone!
        Nor with the mind at all coequal:

Obviously, Goethe associates the question of knowing with the academic world, for which he shows considerable distaste. Entirely gratuitously, for example, he introduces Wagner's successor, that well-known type of academic toady who may haunt the university for most of his ambient career, and Mephistopheles remarks good-naturedly:

6638   Bemooster Herr! Auch ein gelehrter Mann
        Studiert so fort, weil er nicht anders kann.

        Most mossy Sir! Also a learned man
        Continues study, since naught else he can:

Aside from the sharp mockery of "professional scholars," is it possible to summarize what *Faust* has to say about the possibility of knowing? Probably three general remarks can be made: 1) what

commonly passes for knowledge really amounts to mere data which
man must interpret in a meaningful way before it has any value; 2)
man does have, and may even be characterized by, a drive to know;
3) unfortunately, he has a tendency to superimpose his own notions
upon the world, however, and this is dangerous in that he may
become attached to a particular mode of understanding and forget
its hypothetical nature. If we survey all of Goethe's work, including
Faust, in an attempt to come up with a more positive recommenda-
tion to add to these somewhat negative points, then it would probably be one in favor of undoctrinaire acceptance of experience as it
presents itself, constant willingness to interpret experience—but
the drawing of tentative conclusions only:

> Stets geforscht und stets gegründet,
> Nie geschlossen, oft geründet.

> Ever seeking, inferring causes,
> No conclusions, only pauses.

For Goethe, imagination and even fancifulness, but certainly
readiness to accept the hitherto undreamt-of, were indispensable to
the true scientist. In a quite gratuitous outburst against scholars,
Mephistopheles points up their intolerance and unimaginativeness:

4917   Daran erkenn ich den gelehrten Herrn!
     Was ihr nicht tastet, steht euch meilenfern,
     Was ihr nicht faßt, das fehlt euch ganz und gar,
     Was ihr nicht rechnet, glaubt ihr, sei nicht wahr,
     Was ihr nicht wägt, hat für euch kein Gewicht,
     Was ihr nicht münzt, das, meint ihr, gelte nicht!

     By that, I know the learned lord you are!
     What you don't touch, is lying leagues afar;
     What you don't grasp, is wholly lost to you;
     What you don't reckon, think you, can't be true;
     What you don't weigh, it has no weight, alas!
     What you don't coin, you're sure it will not pass.

Goethe himself was very much a creature of his own powerful imagination. We have seen how he claimed for the poet not only the
creative ability to replicate all that nature has to offer, but even to
anticipate experience. This most vital potential in individual identity is the theme which opens *Faust II*.

XII

POETIC
CREATIVITY

ACT I

What is the function of Act I? What is the theme of the colorful
conglomerate? It concludes with Faust's conjuration of Helen—are
we to discover its function here? Surely she could have been
brought into his career with less extravagant effort than that ex-
pended in this longest act of *Faust II*. It may be that Goethe anticipated such questions as ours:

5727   Was solls, ihr Toren? soll mir das?
        Es ist ja nur ein Maskenspaß.

        What ails ye, fools? What mean ye all?
        'T is but a joke of Carnival.

Not merely those who insist on some philosophical idea from *Faust*,
but perhaps also we who would like to perceive some true structural function for each part of the poem should accept answer from
the Herald:

5733   Ihr Täppischen! ein artiger Schein
        Soll gleich die plumpe Wahrheit sein.
        Was soll euch Wahrheit?

        A pleasant cheat, ye dolts! forsooth
        You take at once for naked truth.
        What's truth to you?

THE RIDDLE: 4743 FF.

The first we hear about the Masque is early in the scene "The Emperor's Castle" (4765 ff.) where the Emperor is eagerly looking forward to a carefree pageant. His call for his fool (4728 ff.) provides the first theatrical event of *Faust II:* Mephistopheles as jester comes tumbling in with a riddle:

4743   Was ist verwünscht und stets willkommen?
Was ist ersehnt und stets verjagt?
Was immerfort in Schutz genommen?
Was hart gescholten und verklagt?
Wen darfst du nicht herbeiberufen?
Wen höret jeder gern genannt?
Was naht sich deines Thrones Stufen?
Was hat sich selbst hinweggebannt?

What's cursed and welcomely expected?
What is desired, yet always chased?
What evermore with care protected?
What is accused, condemned, disgraced?
To whom dar'st thou not give a hearing?
Whose name hears each man willingly?
What is 't, before thy throne appearing?
What keeps itself away from thee?

It has been of perennial interest to scholars. They have tried to solve it. The riddle certainly does constitute a crucial part of our introduction to *Faust II*, not because of its solution—it probably does not have any particular solution—but precisely because it challenges us to *solve* it. This puts us in the right mood for the allegories in which Act I, like the remainder of *Faust II*, abounds: all are representations to be solved. Sometimes the solution will be easy, as for the Leviathan of State (5393 ff.); sometimes an enigma will bemuse rather than enlighten, the representation itself appearing more meaningful than whatever it might stand for, like the Mothers (6215 ff.), and we have to do with a symbol. Riddle, allegory, symbol—the frame of mind which all demand of the reader is speculative. He is asked to take counsel with himself (*raten*), now asking what a figure might stand for, now what meaning might playfully lurk behind a mask.

Well, what does Mephistopheles' riddle mean? It appears that the remainder of the scene may be organized in terms of possible answers to his initial challenge. In the first place, of course, Mephistopheles as devil embodies various kinds of answer to his own riddle; but as fool he represents also entertainment, merriment in a larger sense, and allows us to conceive of the entire Masque to come as a possible response to the riddle. This is the charm of all masquerades: who is behind the mask?

But just as soon as the Chancellor offers us an abstract concept, *justice*, we perceive that it meets the terms of Mephistopheles' riddle, too. Indeed, the Chancellor chooses his phrases in such a way as to remind us (4775 ff.) of the riddle's sing-song. The next representative to approach the steps of the throne is the Chief of Staff, and from his words (4812 ff.) we recognize that the *army* or the political *power* it holds out might be yet another solution; the Treasurer advances, and we concede *money* to be an equally apt answer; the Marshal, and we accept *material things* in general as perhaps the best fulfillment so far for all of Mephistopheles' conditions. Now the riddler himself speaks: All these correct answers have boiled down to one, have they not? My riddle represents the multifarious problems of empire, all of which can be met by sufficient wealth (4889 ff.), but this answer is all too easy. Gold is where you find it. The real question is *how* to find it:

4895   Und fragt ihr mich, wer es zutage schafft:
        Begabten Manns Natur- und Geisteskraft!

        And if you ask me who brings it to light:
        The gifted man's nature and mind's insight.

In this way Faust is introduced as the answer to all demands made so far, individually and collectively. The "natural and intellectual powers of a talented man" must, directly or indirectly, provide entertainment, justice, power, wealth, etc., etc.: Faust is the ultimate solution to Mephistopheles' riddle.

By associating the gifted individual with wealth, Mephistopheles has established one major theme of Act I. The next scene, "Spacious Hall," is built up in such a way as to direct our minds toward glittering gold and glittering genius as represented by the central figures of Plutus and Boy Charioteer. "Emperor's Castle" has made it clear that the talents of a gifted man shall be needed to acquire material wealth. The allegory in "Spacious Hall" turns worldy goods toward patronage of human talents. Both scenes together set forth the imaginative individual as source and ultimate justification of material wealth.

SPACIOUS HALL

Now begins the gaiety, now begins the foolishness—the Emperor has been longing for it and his people are grateful for it (5071 ff.). This is a folk festival, and the celebrants are in their costumes. The Garden Girls do not step forward as real gardening girls, but as play actors with artificial flowers:

5100   Allerlei gefärbten Schnitzeln
    Ward symmetrisch Recht getan;
    Mögt ihr Stück für Stück bewitzeln,
    Doch das Ganze zieht euch an.

    Every sort of colored snipping
    Won its own symmetric right:
    Though your wit on each be tripping,
    In the whole you take delight.

Subsequent costumes become more imaginative (olive branch with olives, head of grain, etc.), but we still recognize the citizens wearing them. The imagery becomes less airy and more down to earth (from flower to fruit), cruder segments of the folk appear, but Fancy is constantly heightened. Fancy, not unrelated to foolishness, may be traced back to Mephistopheles' riddle if we like. Here in the bright spectacle of "Spacious Hall" it has become dominant. Not only a poet's fancy is engaged but also that of the citizens in their costumes—and our own fancy is charged with seeing more than the poetry implies, for the stage directions are becoming detailed (after 5177, 5198, 5294, 5298). At last the representations on stage become

so elaborate in the extreme that we cease to be aware of ordinary
citizens behind all the costumes.

The classical masks are subject to especially radical alteration by
Fancy. The Fates have whimsically switched their roles so as to
cancel out the dark traditional duty of Atropos (5305 f.), and the
horrible Furies do not flap forth as the terrifying daughters of night,
but "fair, well-proportioned, friendly, young in years" (5358). When
Hobbes' Leviathan crosses the stage, we may wonder if the pageant
may not even have got beyond the citizens' control. Here State is
guided by Prudence who holds both madcap Hope and foolish Fear
in check, but Ill Will (Zoilo-Thersites) threatens Victory with some
frightful, mysterious force, and we are not sure whether the Herald
is feigning astonishment or is genuinely surprised by an irrational
turn which transcends the Carnival plans (5500 ff.). Irrationality
clearly takes ascendancy as the scene progresses (5508 ff.), for constantly increased engagement of unfettered Fancy is the organizational principle of "Spacious Hall" so far. The folk who were actors at
the outset have become awed spectators now as high allegory assumes command.

The Herald no longer confidently announces events to come, but
offers mere inept description of the unexpected. Wealth and Poetry
interdependent soar onto the scene, but the Herald's account is so
repetitive and superficial (5535 ff.) that Boy Charioteer himself must
help out:

5573   Bin die Verschwendung, bin die Poesie,
            Bin der Poet, der sich vollendet,
            Wenn er sein eigenst Gut verschwendet.
            Auch ich bin unermeßlich reich
            Und schätze mich dem Plutus gleich,
            Beleb und schmück ihm Tanz und Schmaus;
            Das, was ihm fehlt, das teil ich aus.

            I am Profusion, I am Poesy.
            The Poet I, whose perfect crown is sent
            When he his own best goods hath freely spent.
            Yet, rich in mine unmeasured pelf,
            Like Plutus I esteem myself:
            I prank and cheer his festal show
            And whatsoe'er he lacks bestow.

Poetry, according to this allegory, is inextricably bound up with Wealth. That seems to be why it has assumed the name of Boy Charioteer (*Knabe Lenker* = "youthful holder of the reins"). He turns the brace of horses in accordance with the wishes of Plutus, whom he calls "Sovereign":

614   Lenk ich nicht glücklich, wie du leitest?
        Bin ich nicht da, wohin du deutest?

        Canst thou not on my guidance reckon?
        Am I not there, where thou dost beckon?

The two feel dependent on one another and in perfect harmony with each other (5623 ff.).

We are witnessing an allegorical stage representation of patronage, that institution which has in fact allowed for the production of so many of the great poetic works of civilized man. The ideas expressed here are naturally at loggerheads with those of most poets and critics of our day—in the Western world at any rate. Who can conceive of Robert Lowell and the president of General Motors making the exchange 5614-29?—Or should we conceive of its occurring between the president of General Motors and the head of the advertising firm engaged by his board?—Or between Evgeniy Evtushenko and the Party Chairman? Here we have it: the patron of the modern poet is the People, and he writes for them: "The People, Yes." Our analogy, of course, is strained. Boy Charioteer reins the horses in accordance with the will of a patron who is an individual person. The intellectual who writes for the people is free to interpret—even called on to interpret—the will of a great mute mass which may be the unwitting patron.

Alas, the disharmonious breaks in on the latest allegory, too. In context with the rule of sweet reason there appeared malevolent unreason as Zoilo-Thersites; in context with Wealth and Poetry the opposite pole takes on the visage of Greed (5640 ff.), whom the people hate. It is a development which brings about the high point in this central scene of Act I: Plutus perceives Poetry completely free of any context whatever except that of purest Fancy:

5689   Nun bist du los der allzu lästigen Schwere,
        Bist frei und frank: nun frisch zu deiner Sphäre!
        Hier ist sie nicht! Verworren, scheckig, wild
        Umdrängt uns hier ein fratzenhaft Gebild.
        Nur wo du klar ins holde Klare schaust,
        Dir angehörst und dir allein vertraust,
        Dorthin, wo Schönes, Gutes nur gefällt,
        Zur Einsamkeit!—Da schaffe deine Welt!

        Now thou hast left the onerous burden here,
        Thou'rt wholly free: away to thine own sphere!
        Here it is not! Confused and wild, to-day,
        Distorted pictures press around our way.
        Where clear thy gaze in sweet serenity,
        Owning thyself, confiding but in thee,
        Thither, where Good and Beauty are unfurled,
        To Solitude!—and there create thy world!

After Boy Charioteer exits we are left in a progressively less fanciful atmosphere. We discover that we are again aware of the people who are staging the pageant. The Herald regains his composure and confidently reminds us that it is *ja nur ein Maskenspaß*—"just a masque for fun" (5728). In Plutus we think we see Faust (5737); in Greed we recognize Mephistopheles (always interested in a little obscenity—5775 ff.). Pan may mystify us at first, but Faust recognizes him (as the Emperor and his retinue—5807 ff.), and now the poetic theme relates itself at last to the plot: Fancy shows herself capable of producing something eminently practical, certificates of imaginary wealth which, once they bear the Emperor's signature, become bogus money.

In *Faust II* the plot is never so important as the themes. In Act I an important theme is creative Fancy, the only human talent competent to hold such a motley mass as that of "Spacious Hall" together. It constitutes a most important thematic introduction to *Faust II*, in which Fancy continues to be a main ingredient, as well as the major demand on the reader. In its last allegorical representative, Fancy took on face and form of *heilige Poesie*—"sacred poesy" (9863), and this may be the aspect which concerns us during the remainder of Act I.

A GLOOMY GALLERY, BRILLIANTLY LIGHTED HALLS, HALL
OF THE KNIGHTS

In "Gloomy Gallery" Faust is called on to produce. It is made clear that to do so he must draw on his own resources, his creative imagination. Faust's own words as Plutus were our first description of the realm to which he now must turn:

6693   Nur wo du klar ins holde Klare schaust,
        Dir angehörst und dir allein vertraust,
        Dorthin, wo Schönes, Gutes nur gefällt,
        Zur Einsamkeit!—Da schaffe deine Welt!

        Where clear thy gaze in sweet serenity,
        Owning thyself, confiding but in thee,
        Thither, where Good and Beauty are unfurled,
        To Solitude!—and there create thy world!

The extreme importance of solitude for the creative act is not a new topic in *Faust*. It was touched upon in "Dedication" and discussed by the Poet in "Prelude on the Stage" (e.g., 63 ff.). We shall do well to bear in mind such reverential statements about *Einsamkeit*—"solitude"—when we listen now to Mephistopheles describe the realm of the Mothers. It strikes him as one of utter emptiness:

6213   Göttinnen thronen hehr in Einsamkeit,
        Um sie kein Ort, noch weniger eine Zeit.

        In solitude are throned the Goddesses,
        No Space around them, Place and Time still less;

He sees only loneliness and desolation there:

6226   Von Einsamkeiten wirst umhergetrieben.
        Hast du Begriff von Öd und Einsamkeit?

        Through endless solitudes shalt thou be drifted.
        Hast thou through solitudes and deserts fared?

It has been our repeated observation that Mephistopheles' appreciation of a subject is likely to wane in direct proportion to its significance for Faust. As we approach the ideal wellsprings of creativity he speaks in essentially negative terms about the solitude there. As for Faust, he found emptiness when in the company of people:

6231   Mußt ich nicht mit der Welt verkehren?
        Das Leere lernen, Leeres lehren?

        Have I not known all earthly vanities?
        Learned the inane, and taught inanities?

and in solitude he sought his refuge:

6235   Mußt ich sogar vor widerwärtigen Streichen
        Zur Einsamkeit, zur Wildernis entweichen.

        Enforced by odious tricks, have I not fled
        To solitudes and wildernesses?

Mephistopheles is at great pains to make clear what he thinks it must be like for man to be entirely alone (6239 ff.). We shall expect his attitude toward the single most important circumstance of creativity to contrast strongly with Faust's, who is immediately excited, thrilled (6216 f.), and ready to undertake the quest (6222), perhaps momentarily intimidated when he learns the relationship of the key to the Mothers (6265 f.), but inspired again once he has seized the key (6281 f.) and resolute in seeking out the Mothers' solitary abode. We are fortunate that when Faust returns he is remarkably explicit about what he found:

6427   Mütter, die ihr thront
        Im Grenzenlosen, ewig einsam wohnt—
        Und doch gesellig! Euer Haupt umschweben
        Des Lebens Bilder, regsam, ohne Leben.
        Was einmal war, in allem Glanz und Schein,
        Es regt sich dort, denn es will ewig sein.

Ye Mothers, in your name, who set your throne
In boundless Space, eternally alone,
And yet companioned! All the forms of Being,
In movement, lifeless, ye are round you seeing.
Whate'er once was, there burns and brightens free
In splendor—for't would fain eternal be;

The symbol of the Mothers seems to imply that the individual in his
own most private depths can find access to cultural patterns developed during past generations. Life continues to take constant
recourse to them—a "bold magician" is he who can draw upon them
for his own creative purposes:

6433   Und ihr [Mütter] verteilt es [was einmal war], allgewaltige
            Mächte,
        Zum Zelt des Tages, zum Gewölb der Nächte.
        Die einen [des Lebens Bilder] faßt des Lebens holder Lauf,
        Die andern sucht der kühne Magier auf;
        In reicher Spende läßt er, voll Vertrauen,
        Was jeder wünscht, das Wunderwürdige, schauen.

        And you [Mothers] dispense it [what once existed] you omnipotent
            powers,
        To the tent of day, to the vault of nights.
        The sweet progress of life takes some [of life's images].
        The bold magician seeks out others,
        Generously giving and full of confidence, he lets
        Each behold the marvel that each wishes.

The greater part of Act I has gone to developing the theme Fancy
in a lighthearted way, relating it to Poetry, Wealth—and even to the
plot of *Faust II*. Here at the end, the theme is modulated to touch
the creative imagination. This is the way Act I flows into Act II, and
indeed into the remainder of *Faust*. Creativity takes place at the
most intimate node in man, where the chromosomes inherited from
his cultural past are shuffled to yield infinitely varied combinations:
Act I concludes by contrasting the intimacy of the creative experience with the coldness of its impersonal exploitation.

Sexuality is of primary importance in the creative act (I am not
sure that Faust—or Goethe—would be lucidly enough aware of this

point to apply such a specific word). There is a key (6259) by which
alone Faust can gain entry to the Mothers. At first it appears to him
to be a negligible thing, but Mephistopheles knows its powers and
can call attention to them:

6259   MEPHISTOPHELES.   Hier diesen Schlüssel nimm!

     FAUST.   Das kleine Ding!

     MEPHISTOPHELES.   Erst faß ihn an und schätz ihn nicht
     gering!

     FAUST.   Er wächst in meiner Hand! er leuchtet! blitzt!

     MEPHISTOPHELES.   Merkst du nun bald, was man an ihm
     besitzt?
     Der Schlüssel wird die rechte Stelle wittern;
     Folg ihm hinab: er führt dich zu den Müttern!

     MEPHISTOPHELES.   Here, take this key!

     FAUST.   That little thing?

     MEPHISTOPHELES.   Take hold of it, not undervaluing!

     FAUST.   It glows, it shines—increases in my hand!

     MEPHISTOPHELES.   How much 't is worth, thou soon shalt
     understand.
     The Key will scent the true place from all others:
     Follow it down!—'t will lead thee to the Mothers.

To hear him tell it, the key is going to remain crucial during the
entire productive experience. Although it is he who makes Faust
aware of the key, we are not surprised when he admits that he does
not in fact comprehend its potential and is even unsure about the
consequences which its employment may have for Faust:

6305   Wenn ihm der Schlüssel nur zum besten frommt!
     Neugierig bin ich, ob er wiederkommt.

> If only, by the key, he something learn!
> I'm curious to see if he return.

Using the key is a serious business indeed.

"Brightly Lighted Halls" is of course a title chosen for its striking contrast to "Gloomy Gallery": we emerge into illuminated spaciousness and go to witness the public display of that which was evoked in solitude. "Hall of the Knights" is so constructed as to bring out the monstrous disproportion between the attitude of the public toward Helen and Paris, and Faust's own response to the couple. This presentation is the result of the greatest and most serious effort of his life, the unique experience of creativity. The bond between creator and creature is a fragile one, yet overwhelming, so that Act I concludes with his collapse, and therapy must be sought afar.

The whole effort occurred in compliance with a request for light entertainment (6183), and the ostensible result is a superficial kind of distraction for a public which Goethe presents to us in the glaring light of harsh satire. The jejune nobility offer an eloquent illustration of the supercilious prediction which the Comic Character made:

179   Ein jeder sieht, was er im Herzen trägt.

         For each beholds what in his bosom lurks.

We saw that he, too, was aware of the serious, indeed obligatory, bond between poet and poetic creation.

The theme Fancy undergoes many colorful variations from the lighthearted to the deeply problematical, but the progress of Act I can be measured by its constantly heightened seriousness. The culmination is what Goethe apparently felt to be the most intense personal relationship to Fancy which Faust can experience: engagement of his productive imagination to beget its own creatures in its own matrix. Arising as they do out of his cultural lineage, his own creatures prove capable of possessing and even overwhelming the creative personality which evoked them—while the sociable consumers of his work take it all as inconsequential entertainment.

EPILOGUE

This Invitation to *Faust* was conceived as a book which would speak to a few fundamentals, provocatively if possible, but never in an obligatory way and certainly not exhaustively. I have heeded, for example, neither the extraordinary theatrical finesse of the Gretchen drama and equally effective parts of *Faust II*, nor the many lyrical outbursts without compare in German tongue, like the ode to human aspiration *Doch laß uns dieser Stunde schönes Gut* (1068 ff.) and the patriotic hymn to Greece, a land never glimpsed by Goethe, *Und sie beschützen um die Wette* (9510 ff.). After all, the major argument I have sought to make is that these things lie at hand, easily discovered by any reader willing to bring only his human needs and experience to the poem. We have good reason to think that the poet was addressing himself to the generally shared experience of our common existence.

No attempt has been made in these pages to point up the numerous themes which, like veins, course through the great poem and sustain it. Following any one of them—Care, Striving, Becoming, Activism, Love, to name only a few of the best known and most often discussed—can lead to ever new ways of experiencing the entire structure of Faust. In conclusion I do want to touch very briefly on just two especially lyrical themes which tend to support my major contention, *vision* and *woman*. They are perhaps the first recurrent topics which strike a reader who asks himself about the artistry and unity of the poem.

Sight is one of Faust's most characteristic attributes, and it becomes even more pronounced as he gets older, Lynceus' appearances more frequent. It is this Lynceus who opens the last day for Faust with a magnificent visual depiction:

11143   Die Sonne sinkt, die letzten Schiffe,
       Sie ziehen munter hafenein.
       Ein grosser Kahn ist im Begriffe,
       Auf dem Kanale hier zu sein.

Die bunten Wimpel wehen fröhlich,
Die starren Masten stehn bereit.

The sun goes down, the ships are veering
To reach the port, with song and cheer:
A heavy galley, now appearing
On the canal, will soon be here.
The gaudy pennons merrily flutter,
The masts and rigging upward climb.

Overview of all that he has accomplished on the coast is crucial to
any pleasure that Faust might be able to take in it. This is one reason
he envies Philemon and Baucis their hill:

1243   Dort wollt ich, weit unherzuschauen,
        Von Ast zu Ast Gerüste bauen,
        Dem Blick eröffnen weite Bahn,
        Zu sehn, was alles ich getan,
        Zu überschaun mit einem Blick
        Des Menschengeistes Meisterstück.

        There would I, for a view unbaffled,
        From bough to bough erect a scaffold,
        Till for my gaze a look be won
        O'er everything that I have done,
        To see before me, unconfined,
        The masterpiece of human mind.

"Dead of Night" and then "Midnight" become scenes dominated by
the theme, in ironical contrast to their titles. First there is Lynceus'
famous lyric *Zum Sehen geboren;* then follows his visual account,
equally beautiful, of the horrible fire in which Philemon and Baucis
perish. This is the way Goethe introduces that scene in which Faust
must forego his most precious attribute; all is prepared for his last
delusion and the bitter irony of his dying moment.

The terrible impact of Faust's blindness has been prepared for by
the frequent recurrence of visual themes throughout the poem.
Everywhere we notice that objects are being fastened by a sharp,
competent eye—I would make no attempt to enumerate the instances. One of the most famous of the visual passages is the so-

called "Easter Walk," when Faust describes the explosion of his walled town below (916 ff.) into a bright colored flower as the motley citizens pour out at all gates. Among the most beloved and eloquent of the lyrics to sight is that one which opens *Faust II*. Here is an extended treatment of vision emergent, so exquisitely accurate that it does honor even to an author celebrated still for his research in color perception. The poem begins in darkness:

4640   Und den Augen dieses Müden
        Schließt des Tages Pforte zu.

        And upon these eyelids weary
        Shut the golden gates of Day.

Now comes the recognition, so easily forgotten in an industrial age like ours, that only in total darkness can the sacred stars disclose themselves, tiny points in space (4642 ff.). Perception of a point of light occurs at the threshold of vision. With just a little diffused light, as at the approach of dawn (4650 ff.), shapes can emerge as variations in intensity of blackness (4654 f.). A field of grain reflects relatively much light, and this is particularly striking if the breath of air stirred by a new day yet beyond the horizon ripples the heads (4656 f.). Thus rises hope as night ends.

Subsequent stages of emergent vision become the subject of a second lyric (4679 ff.): out of the mists, details take on outline, colors appear, the sun strikes dewdrops. Suddenly the abundance of light overwhelms us. For the world which an unbearable light source displays to our eye we are grateful.

Another of the many highly lyrical themes pervading *Faust* is closely related to man's vision: his love of woman. The splendid aspect of Helen as sung by Lynceus at his first appearance (9218 ff.) is one of the finest tributes in *Faust* to the glory of sight and of feminine beauty. The two fundamental qualities of woman as seen by man are her unbelievably strong appeal to his senses, and her sovereign ability to inspire him idealistically and lead him on toward his noblest ideals. Gretchen may exemplify the one, Helen the other—but at last both qualities are subsumed in redeeming love.

Wherever we find this all-important theme we can usually discern its double significance for Faust—or for man in general. Note, for example, the forthright introduction of woman into the work:

828   Blitz, wie die wackern Dirnen schreiten!

       Deuce! how they step, the buxom wenches!

What male can fail to sympathize with the boys watching the working girls on their day off? But moving more demurely not far behind are the proper daughters of solid citizenry:

840   Sie gehen ihren stillen Schritt
       Und nehmen uns doch auch am Ende mit.

       They go their quiet way
       And will take us along, too, finally.

These two fundamental meanings of femininity for man rise at last after Act III to what I take to be the noblest lyric poem in *Faust*. It might be entitled: Dem Ewig-Weiblichen—"To the Eternal-Feminine."

9039   Der Einsamkeiten tiefste schauend unter meinem Fuß,
       Betret ich wohlbedächtig dieser Gipfel Saum,
       Entlassend meiner Wolke Tragewerk, die mich sanft
       An klaren Tagen über Land und Meer geführt.
       Sie löst sich langsam, nicht zerstiebend, von mir ab.
       Nach Osten strebt die Masse mit geballtem Zug;
       Ihr strebt das Auge staunend in Bewundrung nach.
       Sie teilt sich wandelnd, wogenhaft, veränderlich;
       Doch will sichs modeln.—Ja, das Auge trügt mich nicht!
       Auf sonnbeglänzten Pfühlen herrlich hingestreckt,
       Zwar riesenhaft, ein göttergleiches Fraungebild,
       Ich sehs! Junonen ähnlich, Ledan, Helenen,
       Wie majestätisch-lieblich mirs im Auge schwankt!
       Ach! schon verrückt sichs! Formlos-breit und aufgetürmt
       Ruht es in Osten, fernen Eisgebirgen gleich,
       Und spiegelt blendend flüchtger Tage großen Sinn.

Doch mir umschwebt ein zarter, lichter Nebelstreif
Noch Brust und Stirn, erheiternd, kühl und schmeichelhaft.
Nun steigt es leicht und zaudernd hoch und höher auf,
Fügt sich zusammen.—Täuscht mich ein entzückend Bild
Als jugenderstes, längstentbehrtes höchstes Gut?
Des tiefsten Herzens frühste Schätze quellen auf:
Aurorens Liebe, leichten Schwung bezeichnets mir,
Den schnellempfundnen, ersten, kaum verstandnen Blick,
Der, festgehalten, überglänzte jeden Schatz.
Wie Seelenschönheit steigert sich die holde Form,
Löst sich nicht auf, erhebt sich in den Äther hin
Und zieht das Beste meines Innern mit sich fort.

Down-gazing on the deepest solitudes below,
I tread deliberately this summit's lonely edge,
Relinquishing my cloudy car, which hither bore
Me softly through the shining day o'er land and sea.
Unscattered, slowly moved, it separates from me.
Off eastward strives the mass with rounded, rolling march:
And strives the eye, amazed, admiring, after it.
In motion it divides, in wave-like, changeful guise;
Yet seems to shape a figure.—Yes! mine eyes not err!—
On sun-illumined pillows beauteously reclined,
Colossal, truly, but a godlike woman-form,
I see! The like of Juno, Leda, Helena,
Majestically lovely, floats before my sight!
Ah, now 't is broken! Towering broad and formlessly,
It rests along the east like distant icy hills,
And shapes the grand significance of fleeting days.

Yet still there clings a light and delicate band of mist
Around my breast and brow, caressing, cheering me.
Now light, delayingly, it soars and higher soars,
And folds together.—Cheats me an ecstatic form,
As early-youthful, long-foregone and highest bliss?
The first glad treasures of my deepest heart break forth;
Aurora's love, so light of pinion, is its type,
The swiftly-felt, the first, scarce-comprehended glance,
Outshining every treasure, when retained and held.
Like Spiritual Beauty mounts the gracious Form,

Dissolving not, but lifts itself through ether far,
And from my inner being bears the best away.

It is easy to see why editors sometimes print the poem in two parts. The first sixteen lines pertain to something fantastic and ethereal but nevertheless *objectively* observed: a cloud formation which, for Faust, "reflects the high meaning of days dazzlingly fleeting" (10054). The rest of the poem is very *subjective* memory, called a band of mist which still enshrouds Faust's *Brust und Stirn*—his "heart and mind." This "lovely shape" does not dissolve as did the objectively perceived cloud. Although it rises into the ether it is not lost by the mind's eye which conceives it. As it goes it draws Faust's inner being up with it.

Of course the poem actually falls into three parts. The first four lines inform us of Faust's fantastic journey back from Greece. Then follow twelve lines to the ideal—call it Leda, call it Helen or even Juno (10050), no matter—the perception of classical beauty. Another twelve lines recall youthful, sensual love of woman. It is the nearest reference to Gretchen which we can find in *Faust II*, save at the very end when one of the penitents who "used to be called Gretchen" does indeed draw Faust's inner being up with her.

The poem asserts its central position by gathering various complex thematic strands which pervade *Faust*, so as to convey an important recognition of the poem: our objectively perceived ideals have to do with *this* life; the tender sensualism of love is our truest intimation of immortality. There is a strange and wonderful kind of consonance between this perception by the old man and such emotionally charged expressions of the very young poet as, for example, Faust's famous declaration in "Martha's Garden" (3431 ff.) that his best assurance of the beyond is in the immediate presence of his sweetheart.

So I confess that I, too, have found a message in *Faust*. I expect that many in the science-ridden generations since 1832 have heard it. While abstract constructs of intellect are glorious indeed, the ultimate realities are near at hand, and we can rely on our own perceptions and inner feelings to apprehend them.

WALPURGIS NIGHT DREAM:
FAUST RESEARCH 1964 TO 1974*
WITH BIBLIOGRAPHIC EXCURSUS

Atkins, Stuart. "The interpretation of Goethe's Faust since 1958." *OL*, 20 (1965), 239–267.

Bahr, Ehrhard. *Die Ironie im Spätwerk Goethes; "... diese sehr ernsten Scherze...": Studien zum 'West-östlichen Divan', zu den 'Wanderjahren' und zu 'Faust II'*. Berlin: Erich Schmidt, 1972.

Banerjee, Nandakishore. "Die Faust-Prologe." In: Banerjee, *Der Prolog im Drama der deutschen Klassik: Studien zu seiner Poetik*. Munich: UNI-Druck, 1970. Pl. 122–148.

Barrack, Charles M. "Mephistopheles: Ein Teil von jener Kraft, Die stets das Böse will und stets das Gute Schafft." *Seminar*, 7 (1971), 163–174.

Bietak, Wilhelm. "Homunculus und die Entelechie: Zu Otto Höflers Buch *Homunculus*." *Goethe* 76, (1972), 12–28.

Binder, Alwin. *Das Vorspiel auf dem Theater: Poetologische und Geschichtsphilosophische Aspekte in Goethes Faust-Vorspiel*. Bonn: Bouvier, 1969.

Binder, Wolfgang. "Goethes klassische *Faust*-Konzeption." *DVLG*, 42 (1968), 55–88.

Bluhm, Heinz. "Zur Entstehung und Interpretation der Szene 'Grosser Vorhof des Palasts' in der Fausthandschrift VH². " in: *Traditions and Transitions: Studies in Honor of Harold Jantz*. Ed. Kurth, McClain, Homann. Munich: Delp, 1972. Pp. 142–161.

Blume, Bernhard. "Fausts Himmelfahrt." *Etudes Germaniques*, 22 (1967), 338–345.

Böckmann, Paul. "Die zyklische Einheit der Faustdichtung." In: *Formensprache: Studien zur Literarästhetik und Dichtungsinterpretation*. Hamburg: Hoffmann und Campe, 1966. Pp. 193–209.

Böhm, Wilhelm. *Faust der Nicht-Faustische*. Halle: Niemeyer, 1933.

Brauning-Oktavio, Hermann. "Der Einfluss von Johan Heinrich Mercks Schicksal auf Goethes *Faust* (1774) und *Tasso* (1780/88)." *JFDH* (1962), pp. 9–57.

---

*Abbreviations are those used in the *PMLA International Bibliography*.

Browning, Robert M. "On the Structure of the *Urfaust.*" *PMLA*, 68 (1953), 458–495.

Bub, Douglas F. "The 'Hexenküche' and the 'Mothers' in Goethe's *Faust.*" *MLN*, 83 (1968), 775–779.

———. "The true Prologue to Goethe's *Faust.*" *MLN*, 84 (1969), 791–796.

———. "Im Anfang war das Wort." *GQ*, 47 (1974), 45–51.

Burdach, Konrad. "Faust und die Sorge." *DVLG*, 1 (1923), 1–60.

Chawtassi, Grigori. "Auseinandersetzung mit Benno von Wieses *Faust* Interpretation." *WB*, 12 (1966), 337–351.

Cottrell, Alan P. "Zoilo-Thersites: Another 'Sehr ernster Scherz' in Goethe's *Faust II.*" *MLQ*, 29 (1968), 29–41.

———. "Chalice and Skull: A Goethean Answer to Faust's Cognitional Dilemma." *GQ*, 45 (1972), 4–19.

Dieckmann, Lieselotte. *Goethe's Faust: A Critical Reading.* New Jersey: Prentice-Hall, 1972.

Dietze, Walter. "Der 'Walpurgisnachtstraum' in Goethe's *Faust:* Entwurf, Gestaltung, Funktion." *PMLA*, 84 (1969), 476–491.

———. "Tradition, Gegenwart und Zukunft in Goethes *Faust.*" *Deutschunterricht für Erziehungs- und Bildungsaufgaben*, 24 (1971), 267–285.

Döring, Hellmut. "Homunculus." *WB*, 11 (1965), 185–194.

———. "'Der Schöngestalt bedenkliche Begleiter:' Betrachtungen zu *Faust II*, 3." *WB*, 12 (1966), 261–272.

Dörrie, Heinrich. "Der Triumph der Galatee im *Faust II.*" In: *Die schöne Galatea: Eine Gestalt am Rande des Griechischen Mythos in antiker und neuzeitlicher Sicht.* Munich: Ernst Heimeran, 1968. Pp. 73–76.

Dshinoria, Otar. "Die Beschwörung der Helena in Goethes *Faust.*" *Goethe*, 32 (1970), 91–114.

———. "Das Ende von Goethes *Faust.*" *Goethe*, 90 (1973), 57–106.

Emrich, Wilhelm. *Die Symbolik von Faust II: Sinn und Vorformen.* Bonn: Athenäum, 2nd ed., 1957.

Engelsing, Rolf. "Die Entstehung von Goethes *Faust* in sozialgeschichtlichen Zusammenhang." *CollG*, 6 (1971–72), 126–164.

Flügel, Heinz. "Gericht über *Faust.*" In: Flügel, *Konturen des Tragischen: Exemplarische Gestalten der Weltliteratur.* Stuttgart: Evangelisches Verlagswerk, 1965. Pp. 100–116.

Forster, Leonard. "Lynkeus' masque in *Faust II.*" *GL&L*, 23 (1969/70), 62–71.

———. "Faust and the Sin of Sloth; Mephistopheles and the Sin of Pride." In: *The Discontinuous Tradition: Studies in German Literature in Honor of Ernest Ludwig Stahl.* Ed. Peter Ganz. Oxford: Clarendon Press, 1971. Pp. 54–66.

Franz, Erich. *Mensch und Dämon: Goethes Faust als menschliche Tragödie, ironische Weltschau und religiöses Mysterienspiel.* Tübingen: Max Niemeyer, 1953.

Frykenstedt, Holger. *Goethes Faust. Verket och forskningen.* Stockholm: Norstedt and Söners, 1969.

Fuchs, Albert. "La personalité de Faust." *Bulletin de la Faculté des Lettres de l'Université de Strasbourg,* 40 (1961–62), 499–506. Also in: Fuchs, *Goethe-Studien.* Berlin: Walter de Gruyter & Co., 1968. Pp. 26–41.

———. "Faust et la nature." *Festgabe für L. L. Hammerich: Aus Anlass seines siebzigsten Geburtstages.* 1962, 69–80. Also in: Fuchs, *Goethe-Studien.* Berlin: Walter de Gruyter & Co., 1968. Pp. 53–63.

———. "Mephistophèles: Son essence: Les traits de son caractère: Son intelligence: Sa Tragédie intime: Ses possibilités de salut. *EG,* 20 (1965), 233–242. Also in: Fuchs, *Goethe-Studien.* Berlin: Walter de Gruyter & Co., 1968. Pp. 42–52.

———. "'Les mères' filles de Méphistophèles et initiatrices de Faust: Un triomphe et une défaite, une défaite et un triomphe." *EG,* 21 (1966), 348–364. Also in: "Die 'Mütter:' Eine Mephistopheles-Phantasmagorie: Ein Triumph und eine Niederlage, Eine Niederlage und ein Triumph." *Goethe-Studien.* Berlin: Walter de Gruyter & Co., 1968. Pp. 64–81.

———. "Faust sur le Brocken." In: *Vergleichen und Verändern: Festschrift für Helmut Motekat.* Ed. Albrecht Goetze and Günther Pflaum. Munich: Max Hueber, 1970. Pp. 28–35.

———. "'Helena:' Mit dieser Helena-Analyse wird ein Teil einer angekündigten Gesamtinterpretation des *Faust* vorgelegt," *Recherches Germaniques,* 1 (1971), 101–108.

———. "Zur Theorie und Praxis der Textinterpretation: 'Gretchens Stube: Gretchen am Spinnrade allein.'" In: *Deutsche Weltliteratur von Goethe bis Ingeborg Bachmann: Festgabe für J. Alan Pfeffer.* Tübingen: Max Niemeyer, 1972. Pp. 28–44.

Gellinek, Christian. "A Note to *Faust II:* vv. 11741–11816." *Symposium,* 20 (1966), 113–116.

Goldsmith, Ulrich K. "Ambiguities in Goethe's *Faust:* A Lecture for the General Reader." *GQ,* 39 (1966), 311–328.

Götze, Alfred. "Goethes *Faust* und Madame de Staël." *Archiv.* 204 (1968), 184–191.

Gray, Ronald. "*Faust* Part I and *Faust* Part II." In: *Goethe: A Critical Introduction.* Cambridge: University Press, 1967. Pp. 126–185.

Grumach, Ernst. "Prolog und Epilog im Faustplan von 1797." *Goethe,* 14–15 (1952–53), 63–107.

Hahn, Karl-Heinz. "Faust und Helena oder die Aufhebung des Zwiespalts zwischen Klassikern und Romantikern: Ein Beitrag zur Romantikkritik Goethes im Spiegel der Faustdichtung." *Goethe,* 32 (1970), 115–141.

Hardy, Swana L. *Goethe, Calderón und die romantische Theorie des Dramas.* Heidelberg: Carl Winter, 1965.

Hass, Hans Egon. "Über die Ironie bei Goethe." In: *Ironie und Dichtung.* Ed. Albert Schaefer, Munich: Beck, 1970. Pp. 59–84.

Heiseler, Bernt von. "Die 'Kerkerszene' in der ursprünglichen und in der endgültigen Gestalt." In: Heiseler, *Gesammelte Essays zur alten und neuen Literatur.* Stuttgart: Steinkopf, 1966. Pp. 54–64.

Heller, Erich. "Fausts Verdammnis: Die Ethik des Wissens." *Merkur,* 17 (1963), 32–56.

Henning, Hans. "Goethe-Bibliographie 1970" et seq. In: *Goethe,* 89 (1972) and subsequent volumes (before 1972 by Heinz Nicolai).

————. *Faust-Bibliographie: Teil II.* 2 vols. Berlin: Aufbau Verlag, 1970.

Hippe, Robert. "Der 'Walpurgisnachtstraum' in Goethes *Faust:* Versuch einer Deutung." *Goethe,* 28 (1966), 67–75.

Höfler, Otto. *Homunculus: Eine Satire auf A. W. Schlegel: Goethe und die Romantik.* Wien-Köln-Graz: Hermann Böhlau, 1972.

Holtzhauer, Helmut. "Aufklärung, Kunst und Faust: Der Übergang vom ersten zum zweiten Teil der Tragödie." *WB,* 9 (1963), 275–294.

————. "*Faust,* Signatur des Jahrhunderts: Eine Analyse der Welt- und Menschenansicht Goethes in seinem Hauptwerk," *Goethe,* 32 (1970), 1–28.

Jantz, Harold. "Patterns and Structures in *Faust:* A preliminary inquiry." *MLN,* 83 (1968), 359–389.

————. *The Mothers in* Faust: *The Myth of Time and Creativity.* Baltimore: Johns Hopkins, 1969.

————. "Goethe's Last Jest in *Faust* or *Faust holt den Teufel.*" In: *Festschrift für Detlev W. Schumann zum 70. Geburtstag.* Ed. Albert R. Schmitt. Munich: Delp, 1970. Pp. 166–172.

————. "Sense in Nonsense: The Mathematics of Faust's Rejuvenation." *MLN,* 85 (1970), 383–385.

Jaszi, Andrew. *Entzweiung und Vereinigung: Goethes symbolische Weltanschauung.* Heidelberg: Lothar Stiehm. 1973.

Kalmbach, Heide. *Bildung und Dramenform in Goethes "Faust".* Göppingen: Kümmerle, 1974.

Keller, Werner. *Goethes Dichterische Bildlichkeit: Eine Grundlegung.* Munich: Fink, 1972.

Kleiner, Juliusz. "Persönlichkeit und überpersönliche Werte in Goethes *Faust.*" *Michkiewicz-Blätter,* 13 (1968), 97–107.

Koch, Friedrich. "Christliches und Scheinchristliches in Goethes *Faust.*" *GRM*, 47 (1966), 244–263.

Lengefeld, Wilhelm Kleinschmidt von. "Goethes *Faust:* Tragödie oder Fabel-dichtung?" *JFDH* (1970), 98–126.

Levedahl, Kathrun Scates. "The Witch's One-times one: Sense or Nonsense?" *MLN*, 85 (1970), 380–383.

Loeb, Ernst. *Die Symbolik des Wasserzyklus bei Goethe.* Paderborn: Schöningh, 1967. Pp. 133–194.

Maché, Ulrich. "Zu Goethes *Faust:* Studierzimmer I und Geisterchor." *Euphorion*, 65 (1971), 200–205.

Mahal, Günther. *Mephistos Metamorphosen.* Göppingen: Kummerle, 1972.

Malsch, Wilfried. "Die Einheit der Faust-Dichtung Goethes in der Spiegelung ihrer Teile." *Festschrift für Klaus Ziegler.* Ed. Catholy. Tübingen: Max Niemeyer, 1968. Pp. 133–158.

Marache, Maurice. "Frederike Brion et l'Urfaust." *Revue d'Allemagne,* 3 (1971), 179–186.

Mason, Eudo C. *Goethe's Faust: Its Genesis and Purport.* Berkeley and Los Angeles: University of California, 1967.

Mayer, Hans. "Der Famulus Wagner und die moderne Wissenschaft." In: *Gestaltungsgeschichte und Gesellschaftsgeschichte: Literatur-, Kunst- und Musikwissenschaftliche Studien.* Ed. Helmut Kreuzer. Stuttgart: J. B. Metzler, 1969. Pp. 176–200.

Meyer, Herman. *Diese sehr ernsten Scherze: Eine Studie zu Faust II.* Poesie und Wissenschaft, 19. Heidelberg: Lothar Stiehm, 1970.

Michelsen, Peter. "Fausts Erblindung." *DVLG*, 36 (1962), 26–35.

Milch, Werner. "Wandlung der Faustdeutung." *ZDP*, 71 (1951–52), 23–38.

Mommsen, Katharine. *Natur- und Fabelreich in Faust II.* Berlin: Walter de Gruyter & Co., 1968.

Müller, Günther. "Goethe-Literatur seit 1945." *DVLG*, 26 (1952), 119–148, 377–410.

Müller Joachim. *Die Figur des Homunculus in der Faustdichtung.* Sitzungsberichte der Sächsischen Akademie der Wissenschaften zu Leipzig, Philologisch-historische Klasse, 108 (1963). Also in: Müller, *Neue Goethe-Studien.* Halle: Max Niemeyer, 1969. Pp. 189–207.

―――. *Prolog und Epilong zu Goethes Faustdichtung.* In: Sitzungsberichte der Sächsischen Akademie den Wissenschaften zu Leipzig, Philologisch-historische Klasse, 110 (1964). Also in: Müller, *Neue Goethe-Studien.* Halle: Max Niemeyer, 1969. Pp. 153–166.

―――. "'Meiner Wolke Tragewerk:' Fausts Abschied von Helena." In:

Sprachkunst als Weltgestaltung: Festschrift für Herbert Seidler. Salzburg-München, 1966, 172–190. Also in Müller, *Neue Goethe-Studien.* Halle: Max Niemeyer, 1969. Pp. 209–224.

———. "Fausts Tat und Tod: Umriss einer Motivanalyse." *Goethe*, 29 (1967), 139–165. Also in: Müller, *Neue Goethe-Studien.* Halle: Max Niemeyer, 1969. Pp. 167–188.

———. *Zur Motivstruktur von Goethes Faust.* Sitzungsberichte der Sächsischen Akademie der Wissenschaften zu Leipzig, Philologisch-historische Klasse, 116 (1972).

Müller-Seider, Walter. "Lynkeus: Lyrik und Tragik in *Faust.*" In: *Sprache und Bekenntnis: Sonderband des Literaturwissenschaftlichen Jahrbuchs: Hermann Kunisch zum 70. Geburtstag.* Ed. by W. Früwald and Günter Niggl. Berlin: Duncker & Humbolt, 1971. Pp. 79–100.

Nauhaus, Wilhelm, "Des bunten Bogens Wechseldauer." *Goethe*, 28 (1966), 106–121.

Neumann, Harry. "Goethe's Faust and Plato's Glaucon: The political necessity for philosophy." *SG*, 19 (1966), 627–632.

Nollendorfs, Valters. *Der Streit um den Urfaust.* The Hague and Paris: Mouton & Co., 1967.

Ost, Hans. "Goethes Helena als plastische Gestalt." *Arcadia*, 4 (1969), 16–42.

Otto, Regine. "Herder-Wirkungen im Urfaust.: *Goethe*, 32 (1970), 50–54.

———. "Kolloquium über Goethes Faust in Weimar." *WB*, 16 (1970), 193–196.

Paul, Fritz. "Gebirge und Meer in der Szenerie des 4. Aktes von *Faust II.*" *OL*, 25 (1970), 230–243.

Peterich, Eckart. "Die drei Erzengel in Goethes 'Prolog im Himmel.'" *LJGG*, 8 (1967), 305–309.

Petzsch, Hans. "Wenn es noch lebt, irrt in der Welt zerstreuet." *Goethe*, 28 (1966), 318–320.

Pinette, Gaspard L. "Ariels Gesang und die Musica Mundana." In: *Vergleichen und Verändern: Festschrift für Helmut Motekat.* Ed. Albrecht Goetze and Günther Pflaum. Munich: Max Hueber, 1970. Pp. 36–43.

Politzer, Heinz. "Vom Baum der Erkenntnis und der Sünde der Wissenschaft: Zur Vegetationssymbolik in Goethes *Faust.*" *JDSG*, 9 (1965), 346–372.

Rehder, Helmut. "Tetradic Structure in Goethe's Faust." *GR*, 38 (1963), 52–65.

———. "Entwurf zu einer Einführung in Goethes Faust." In:*Festschrift für Detlev W. Schumann.* Ed. Albert Schmitt. Munich: Delp, 1970. Pp. 145–165.

Requadt, Paul. "Die Figur des Kaisers im Faust II." JDSG, 8 (1964), 153–171.

———. Goethes Faust I: Leitmotivik und Architektur. Munich: Wilhelm Fink, 1972.

Rüdiger, Horst. "Curiositas und Magie: Apuleius und Lucius als literarische Archetypen der Faust-Gestalt." In: Wort und Text: Festschrift für Fritz Schalk. Ed. Harri Meier und Hans Sckommodau. Frankfurt am Main: Vittorio Klostermann, 1963. Pp. 57–82.

———. "Weltliteratur in Goethes 'Helena.'" JDSG, 8 (1964), 172–198.

———. "Hier ist das Wohlbehagen erblich: Goethes Huldigung vor der Liebesdichtung im Helena-Akt. Die Bühnengnossenschaft, 16 (1964), 384–386.

Runge, Edith A. "Osterchor und Geistergesang." In: Wert und Wort: Festschrift für Else M. Fleissner. Ed. Sonnenfeld et al. New York: Wells College, 1965. Pp. 1–8.

Salm, Peter. "Faust, Eros and Knowledge." GQ., 39 (1966), 329–339.

———. The Poem as Plant: A Biological View of Goethe's Faust. Cleveland & London: Western Reserve Press, 1971.

Scheibe, Siegfried. "Zur Entstehung der 'Walpurgisnacht' im Faust I." In: Goethe-Studien: Sitzungsberichte der deutschen Akademie der Wissenschaften zu Berlin, 4 (1965), 7–61.

———. "'Un sac rempli de petits chiffons de papier:' Zu den Papiertaschen von Dichtung und Wahrheit und dem frühen Faust." Goethe, 29 (1967), 166–190.

———. "Bermerkungen zur Entstehungsgeschichte des frühen Faust." Goethe, 32 (1970), 61–71.

———. "Zum Faustparalipomenon 10." Goethe, 33 (1971), 147–156.

———. "Noch einmal zum bezifferten Faustschema von 1797." Goethe, 89 (1972), 235–255.

Schmitz, Hermann. Goethes Altersdenken im problemgeschichtlichen Zusammenhang. Bonn: Bouvier, 1959.

Scholz, Gerhard. Faust-Gespräche. Berlin: Verlag Junge Welt, 1967.

Schulze, Horst. "Das bezifferte Faustschema von 1797." Goethe, 32 (1970), 72–90.

———. "Zum bezifferten Faustschema: Nachtrag und Ergänzung." Goethe, 89 (1972), 256–260.

Schümann-Heinke, Elke. "Die Lichtsymbolik in Faust II." In: Studien zu Goethes Alterswerken. Ed. Erich Trunz. Frankfurt am Main: Athenaum, 1971. Pp. 251–324.

Schüpbach, Werner. Die Menschwerdung als zentrales Phänomen der

Evolution in Goethes Darstellung der Klassischen Walpurgisnacht.
Freiburg: Die Kommenden, 1967.

Schwerte, Hans. *Faust und das Faustische: Ein Kapitel deutscher Ideologie.*
Stuttgart: Ernst Klett, 1962.

Stapf, Paul. "Eine Schillerparodie in Goethes *Faust.*" *Kentucky Foreign Language Quarterly,* 12 (1965), 55–61.

Steffensen, Steffen. "Makrokosmoszeichen und Erdgeist in Goethes *Faust.*" *Kopenhagener germanistische Studien,* 1 (1969), 186–197.

Stelzmann, Rainulf. "Goethe, Friedrich Schlegel und Schleiermacher: Eine verhüllte Kritik im 'Walpurgisnachtstraum.'" *Archiv,* 203 (1967), 195–203.

Stock, F. "Vom Ariel in Shakespeares 'The Tempest' zum Ariel in Goethes *Faust II.*" *Arcadia,* 7 (1972), 274–280.

Streicher, Wolfgang. *Die dramatische Einheit von Goethes Faust: Betrachtet unter den Kategorien Substantialität und Funktionalität.*
Tübingen: Max Niemeyer, 1966.

Streurman, G. H. "Was Faust 'ein guter Mensch?'" *Levende Talen,* 229–232 (1965), 207–216.

Volkmar, Gudrun. "Gretchen und ihre Umwelt." *Theater der Zeit.* 26 (1971), 41–42.

Wachsmuth, Andreas B. "Die Faustgestalt Goethes." In: *Das Menschenbild in der Dichtung.* Ed. Albert Schaefer. Munich: Beck, 1965. Pp. 118–151.

Walsche, O'Connell. "Parzival and Faust." In: *Mélanges pour Jean Fourquet.* Ed. P. Valentin and G. Zink. Paris: Klincksieck; Munich: Hueber, 1969. Pp. 363–370.

Weisinger, Kenneth, D. "A Note on Homunculus, Thales and Anaxagoras." *Monatshefte,* 64 (1972), 237–246.

Wertheim, Ursala. "Der neue Lynkeus: Nachtrag zu den 'Faustgesprächen': Aspekte der Goethe-Rezeption bei Louis Fürnberg." In: *Studien zur Literaturgeschichte und Literaturtheorie.* Ed. Hans-Günther Thalheim, Ursula Wertheim. Berlin: Rütten & Loening, 1970. Pp. 201–221.

Weyl, Shalom, "Ascent and Descent: Some Parallels between Faust's Salvation and the 'Walpurgisnacht.'" *PEGS,* 41 (1971), 91–102.

Wiese, Benno von. *Die deutsche Tragödie von Lessing bis Hebbel.* Hamburg: Hoffmann und Campe, 1958. Pp. 127–189.

Wieszner, Georg Gustav. *Goethes Faust: Ein geistiger Überblick.*
Nürnberg: Hans Carl, 1968.

Wilkinson, Elizabeth M. "Faust in der Logosszene: Willkürlicher Übersetzer oder geschulter Exeget?" *Internationaler Germanistenkongress, Akten*, 4 (1971), 116–124.

———. "Goethe's *Faust:* Tragedy in the diachronic mode." *PEGS*, 42 (1971–72), 116–174.

Willoughby, L. A. "Goethe's *Faust*, a Morphological Approach." In: E. M. Wilkinson and L. A. Willoughby. *Goethe: Poet and Thinker*. London: Barnes & Noble, 1962. Pp. 95–117.

Wittkowski, Wolfgang. "'Gedenke zu leben!' Schuld und Sorge in Goethes *Faust*." *PEGS*, 38 (1967/68), 114–145.

———. "Faust und der Kaiser: Goethes Letztes Wort zum *Faust*." *DVLG*, 43 (1969), 631–651.

Zimmermann, Rolf Christian. *Das Weltbild des Jungen Goethe: Studien zur hermetischen Tradition des deutschen 18. Jahrhunderts*. Munich: Wilhelm Fink, 1969.

"So much has been said about Shakespeare by now that it might seem as though there were nothing left to say; yet it is the nature of intellect eternally to stimulate the intellect." Goethe's opening remark in an essay on Shakespeare takes into account that each age must come to grips with the past on its own terms. Just as the history of Shakespeare criticism is a facet of the history of the European intellect, our vast stores of Goethe research constitute one of our most revealing bodies of source material in the recent history of the German mind. He who steeps himself in these writings does so at his own peril and must recognize that he is pursuing an inquiry quite distinct from the study of Goethe.

Any neophyte should be assured that the Bible, *Phaidros, Hamlet,* and other works which, like *Faust*, have gone to make up the Western mentality are likely to be more informative about *Faust* than any of the writings listed above. He needs also to be forewarned about the heavy pathos which has characterized Goethe criticism; those who take it seriously, like those who recoil from it, can be reminded that the object of their deference or mockery is not Goethe at all, but a monument in his name. It was of the monument that Professor Spranger spoke at the Tübingen celebration of the poet's 200th birthday: "It is necessary that we have undergone a major metamorphosis beyond our own daily existence before we can at all survey the spheres wherein a spirit like Goethe resides." German *Faust* scholarship has been especially successful in convincing the world that Goethe is, as Professor Spranger declares, far removed from our daily existence (the Spranger speech was recently published in an anthology of the best in Goethe criticism).

Faust itself may be partly responsible for this situation. Goethe's treatment of the theme was such as to turn it into a kind of German national myth from the outset. An early "New Critic," he himself well understood that a work of art begins a life of its own just as soon as the artist releases it, and he encouraged readers to allow a world of their own interpretive fantasy to rise up from his writings—*Ein jeder sieht, was er im Herzen trägt* ("For each beholds what in his bosom lurks"). Friedrich Schelling early confirmed this quality: "This poem is no less than the innermost, purest essence of our age: substance and form created from what the times contained and even from what they forebode. Hence it may be called a true mythological poem" (quoted by Schwerte, p. 289). As the Germans fulfilled Schelling's prophecy and persisted in recognizing "the purest essence" of each passing age in the poem, a "Faustian Spirit," drawing its power and appeal from Goethe's work, took on a ghostly existence of its own—and this Goethe probably could not have foreseen.

Much as certain ancient myths are said to go back to learned interpretations—often as not erroneous ones—of yet older ikons, the "Faustian" fabric was woven by generations of German academics, for whom it came to symbolize all kinds of social, political, racial and moral notions. Already the Romantic, Franz Horn, exclaimed: "By no means should we speak of a single poet as originater of this profoundly allegorical legend, but may safely declare that the entire nation has helped to produce it" (quoted by Schwerte, pp. 55 f.). Not until our own century was progress to be made in separating Goethe's work from that myth produced by an entire nation. Wilhelm Böhm, one of the most influential writers against so-called Faustian man, called him "a true Homunculus . . . concocted in the test tube" (p. 83), and Hans Schwerte at last wrote the history of the phantom. It teaches, if nothing else, that each age entertains a highly subjective image of the past.

With what justification then do I conclude a study of *Faust* with a report on *Faust* scholarship? I have tried to answer the question with the report's title. "Walpurgis Night Dream" does not pertain primarily to Faust's own fantasies, but it does inform us of some of the fugitive thoughts in the mind of the author and helps to knit the larger work to its own place and time. Similarly, the issues of *Faust* scholarship serve very well to illustrate the problematic situation of literature studies in our day. In pointing up the main lines in *Faust* scholarship, I shall not try to name every item which has appeared in the past ten years (with Hans Henning's beautifully organized bibliography it is an easy matter to find all written on any subject, even in any particular year). Many items—especially, alas, in the United States where college administrative officers, themselves not actively literate, are

required to exact publications from faculties—are without clearly formulated rationale. In Germany, too, the day has passed in which major Goethe
scholars might be shipbuilders (Max Morris), ministers of state (Gustav von
Loeper), or philosophers (Heinrich Rickert) deeply convinced of poetry's
importance in their people's culture. Writers considered in the following
pages are mostly guildsmen, and a large portion of any one article goes to
settling accounts with the guild.

One of the major problems overshadowing all these writers is precisely
that of a rationale for the guild itself. Of the three scholars who explicitly
turn to clientele (students) as justification for their work, two are women.
While Lieselotte Dieckmann and E. M. Wilkinson (1971–72) place high
demands on their students and certainly expect them to accept unconven-
tional interpretations, Dieckmann, like Ulrich Goldsmith, does seem to feel
that writing for them may amount to something less than writing for fellow
professionals. Wilkinson, on the other hand, is clearly predicating both
rationale and method on her students' own culture.

RÉSUMÉS OF RESEARCH

Werner Milch, Günther Müller and Stuart Atkins (1965) are guides to
work before 1965, and a sequel to Müller has been announced by Ehrhard
Bahr. Valters Nollendorfs and Eudo C. Mason turn out to be excellent
counsel for much of this literature, although my own comments tend to
bring out their few shortcomings more than their considerable merits. Such
books forfeit any independent approach to the work itself as they take their
organization from the willy-nilly of scholarship. For example, the focus of
work on the so-called *Urfaust* has been on questions of genesis and chronol-
ogy; in reporting, Nollendorfs has no choice but to concern himself with
these issues. In his immersion in largely positivistic writings, he himself
comes to accept some of their tacit assumptions, not only about the subject
under discussion but even about the nature of scholarship. Many earlier
researchers postulated an outer world of fairly solid fact, where clearcut
answers can be extracted for all reasonable questions. Were the earliest
Faust writings in coherent MS form or, as some report, "a bag full of
scraps"? Nollendorfs tends to take sides on questions like this, which are not
mutually exclusive.

Nollendorfs' other failing is his acceptance of the term *Urfaust* as designating "the entire written and conceptual state of *Faust* from Goethe's
pre-Italian period" (p. 17) as well as the Göchhausen manuscript—indeed,
in that he speaks of the *Urfaust* "conception," as designating a work in its
own right. The *Urfaust* is, of course, just a scholarly figment, much like the

either theory concocted in the physics laboratories of the 19th century. Our difficulty in literary scholarship, and the reason we have to be so much more self-critical than our colleagues in the sciences, is that we have no empirical *tertium comparationis* to keep us honest. The value of a work like Nollendorfs' is that it brings such issues out into discussion and bares some of our fundamental dilemmas. For example, while we must in good faith read our fellow scholars, Nollendorfs shows that scholarly discussions are not always carried on in behalf of clarification. Eudo C. Mason even argues effectively that many *Faust* hypotheses were set up for the sake of the hypotheses themselves, and served no further end. Mason clears the air of many far-fetched conjectures, such as the dating of portions of the Göchhausen MS on stylistic, linguistic, or biographical bases, and he has simplified our perception of *Faust* decisively.

He feels that Goethe's intent remained essentially the same from the early stages of composition right on through to Faust's salvation (but he does not argue a positive view of Faust, whom Goethe both glorifies and denounces); and he sees the religious views in *Faust I* as those familiar in contemporary German society and not—as some still argue—opaque to all not familiar with cabbalistic writing. Oriented as his work is in accordance with the contours of *Faust* scholarship over recent decades, Mason like Nollendorfs may dwell on matters much discussed by scholars but not really very important. When emphasis goes to questions of compositional history, the earliest parts written get greatest attention. Mason declares that "the *Urfaust* . . . must necessarily be the basis for our understanding of the entire *Faust* drama" (p. 93)—as for *Faust II*, he skips over everything except Act. V.

In all the résumés of research, the reader is liable to lose sight of the woods for the trees—indeed the résuméer himself may overemphasize the trivial, as in Mason's argument that, since Gretchen calls out at the end of the Göchhausen MS: "We'll meet again," and since *she* is obviously going to Heaven, Goethe must have been intending all along to save Faust. What difference does it really make whether the young Goethe had reached a decision one way or another about heaven and hell? Mason is doing what he himself eloquently condemns, setting up an unverifiable, useless hypothesis—and in so doing making the tacit assumption that Gretchen bespeaks not only Goethe's conclusions but the dear Lord's as well. I do not make these remarks in order to ridicule the late Professor Mason, but rather to touch again our central dilemma. Mason had no choice but to involve himself in what his fellow scholars had to say, but like most of us he was unable to do so without bogging his reader down in trivia. Here is evidence that he temporarily lost his own bearings as well. How can that be avoided?

I believe that Professor Mason faced up to the question and found a kind of imperfect answer: keeping our audience in mind is the best way to avoid the trivial and to focus on issues of interest to someone, anyhow. Obviously hoping for a larger audience than merely those who can read German, he translates all quotations; yet at the same time distrusting the generosity of his fellow guildsmen, he offers the same quotations in the original, too, so that we can check up on him. An audience who cannot read *Faust* in the original is not very likely to trace these tedious disputes, but the point is that Mason did show a desire to reach that "general audience." His failure points up the major problem of scholarship in our time.

INTERPRETATIONS OF *Faust*—CONTENT

Over the years *Faust* has proved unusually susceptible to moralistic interpretations. This very quality may account for its high place in the esteem of successive generations able to find in it their own changing aspirations. By and large this ceased to be the case in the West about forty years ago as critics began to stress Faust's unheroic qualities. In our own time few continue to belabor the point, but there are still a few echoes of Wilhelm Böhm. G. H. Streurman holds firm to Faust's actual deeds and judges them in the cold light of Dutch Calvinism to conclude that God was not justified in calling him "a good man." The least He could have done would have been to come forth in person in the final scene instead of dispensing redeeming grace through the Mary cult. Similarly, Friedrich Koch finds Faust's salvation only pseudo-Christian. Heinz Flügel suggests that Goethe himself was uncertain and "confusing" (p. 116) about Faust's end—"But who would expect the poet to be the best critic of his poetry?" (p. 103). The famous translation scene, emphasizing the deed, is an inspiration of the devil. "Are we not obligated to the poet and even to ourselves to defend the original tragic conception of the story against the conciliatory older Goethe and the Faustologues whom he inspired, so that Faust is not a model, but a warning to us?" (p. 110). Ronald Gray attempts a critical treatment of *Faust* for his countrymen—surely striking thus the most rewarding posture for a humanist—but at the same time going along with German views. A recapitulation of Faust's deeds interpreted as ethical development leaves Gray himself frankly nonplussed at the end. This kind of moralistic sitting in judgment on a mere dramatic character is probably as inappropriate for our time as that older view of Faust as a model of constant and eventually rewarded striving.

Heinz Politzer takes up the sinful implications of knowledge raised earlier by Erich Heller. The tree of knowledge is "the emblem of Faust's fate" (p. 359), Philemon and Baucis' grove "the last image of natural order against which Faust has rebelled his life long" (p. 367). "These lindens are images of Faust's fate as such" (p. 369)—yet Politzer will not subscribe to a theological or moralistic interpretation of all this and avers that he is illustrating the conflict between classic and romantic in the vegetable symbolism. A somewhat better balanced attempt to come to terms with these questions is by the philosopher Harry Neumann: "Faust's dilemma is that of a man determined to act nobly, yet unaware of any rational basis for his aspirations" (p. 628). Neumann draws the lesson that "creation of choice of one's values is an act of personal freedom which dictates to reason rather than obeying it" (p. 632). Very rare in the West is that entirely positive interpretation of Faust so familiar from the aggressively bourgeois epoch of our grandfathers. Juliusz Kleiner sees Faust as an aristocratic, religious personality concerned with his own ideal development and rising in Part II to the pinnacle of creativity by means of "creative assimilation." It would be interesting to learn whether Kleiner—apparently a Polish refugee—was intentionally parodying the motto of doctrinaire Marxist criticism.

In any case, the old perfectabilistic Faust concept is still going strong in the East, where "creative assimilation" of the "chief work of German national literature" is the declared purpose which, e.g., Regine Otto (WB, 1970) unabashedly admits to be "intransigently partisan" (pp. 193 and 196). Russian scholarship sometimes bridles at this, e.g., Igor Solotusski condemns Faust in a kind of distillation of all that has been said against "Faustian" man (according to Dshinoria, 1973) but by and large the Marxists are apparently committed to affirming Faust's career as carrying him on to ever nobler heights. This may simply be a result of Party insistence on optimistic literature, but it strikes one as a fusty adherence to views of 19th-century scholars whose Faust interpretations—like all interpretations—mirrored their own culture. Literary scholarship in its most vital phase must spin its web ever anew, its most valuable product its most ephemeral one.

But the Marxists have not swept away the cobwebs of nationalistic, perfectabilistic, expansionistic Faust criticism. Grigori Chawtassi, although subjecting the inner contradictions of Benno von Wiese to scathing criticism, goes ahead to voice the same perfectabilistic Faust view familiar from Ernst Cassirer (1916), Fritz Strich (1928), Eugen Kühnemann (1930), Philipp Witkop (1931), Wilhelm Linden (1932), Heinrich Rickert (1932), etc., but in modern jargon: "While the progressive significance of the bourgeois revolution is recognized [in Faust] it also shows that the victory of bourgeois affairs will sharpen social conflicts and bring about new forms of exploitation of man by man. And, just as in other works, in Faust too the injustice of antagonistic class society is held up to the future ideal of a free humanity . . . Faust steps forward as herald of these progressive views . . . a man striving to achieve a happy existence for all mankind" (pp. 348 ff.). Another Russian, Otar Dshinoria (1973), probably supplies the most helpful résumé and critique of Marxist *Faust* commentary "in the light of current ideological discussions" (p. 73), which see Faust developing in accordance with Goethe's "materialistic-dialectic" thought. "Between the third and fourth act" (p. 74) Faust gives up individualism and becomes a "modest working man" but not a "Philistine business man" (p. 77). Most striking perhaps is Dshinoria's detailed, five-page justification of Faust's part in the deaths of Philemon and Baucis: "The heart of the conflict lies in the fact that the 'conservative' stubbornness of Baucis is in fundamental contradiction of Faust's revolutionary *work*, whereby the tragic turn of this collision symbolizes not only the condemnation of the advocates of the 'old' but also the decisive factor in the development of the 'new hero', his final testing" (p. 81). For Dshinoria (1970), Helen constitutes one of the several temptations along the upward path to truth (p. 102). While she does represent a higher, more spiritualized plane than Gretchen (p. 102), she is too far removed from reality and symbolizes Faust's two errors: individualism and a weakness for metaphysics. Euphorion's death demonstrates the falseness of the Helen liaison.

One's tendency is naturally to ignore the crassest in East German scholarship, much as we cast our eyes down at some gross, but inadvertent breach of etiquette. Walter Dietze (1971) calls *Faust* "probity-fate of man therefore, seen in most general terms; challenge to his moral potentialities, liberation of his history-forming power, development of his humane essence-forces on all sides in the structure built through dialectic conflict" (p. 267). It is "entirely and thoroughly harmoniously, both a sharply negative critique of society and at the same time an incisively positive plan for society" (p. 273). Gerhard Scholz, in a ragout of parallels drawn from numerous other Goethe works and quotations, the intent of which he adjusts with bizarre and tacit use of italics (e.g., pp. 35, 41), once again demonstrates that there are no limits to the possible interpretations of a complex art work. His authoritarian tone may serve as an emphatic reminder that a critic's true task must be to *elicit* interpretation, but never to serve as official guard at the temple of certainty.

Not all Marxist criticism is bad. Helmut Döring, Karl-Heinz Hahn, and Ursula Wertheim connect *Faust* with sociopolitical and ideological issues in such a way as to expand at least the outsider's appreciation, even though such views may exert a more restrictive influence on the Marxist mentality. Joachim Müller obviously wishes to be read by students of literature in the West and has gone so far in approaching Western methodology as to draw an official-sounding reproach from Regine Otto (*WB*, 1970). After a some-

what tedious recapitulation of the Homunculus plot (1963), his contribution
to history of composition (1964) focuses on 1797–98 and the influence of
Schiller, willingly entering into "the artistic organization of the entirety, the
question of the function of prologue and epilogue" (p. 164). Müller explores
symbolism (1966), interpreting the clouds at the beginning of Act IV as
Helen and Gretchen's elevation of Faust beyond the despair of separation
so that he can carry the gain of feminine experience over into "supra-
personal effectiveness" (p. 190). Müller addresses motif analysis (1967),
following the theme of the "deed" and showing it to be a positive reply to
Mephistopheles' defamation of man. Faust is eternally unsatisfied, hence
worthy of salvation because even in death he looks toward yet nobler accomplishments. Müller offers credible replies to reservations published in
the West, e.g., he answers the negative delineation of Faust's personality
by pointing to the dialectic relationship between good and evil. Faust over-
comes the "cheap" temptation of sensual pleasure in favor of democratic
leadership *among* a free people: "Behind the tragic fall glows hope for the
future. Beyond death and devil human perfectability is visible" (188). But
Müller is a structuralist at heart, preferring to seek artistic unity in *Faust* in
terms of intertwined motifs (1972). He is highly successful at following key
words like *Irren, Schauer, Kraft, Kerker, Augenblick*, etc. and showing
them to be rich in associations. Eloquent testimony to his diplomatic han-
dling of doctrine-related issues is his deft division of *Faust* into a character
tragedy (thus going along with post-Wiese Westerners) but at the same time
a "humanity drama" which is optimistic, a "comedy" (Germans are notorious for their assumption that tragedies are sad, comedies happy). Since
Müller approaches so closely to Paul Böckmann's essay on *Faust II* (1966), it
seems to be a striking comment on the state of our scholarly community that
Müller did not receive it until 1971.

    While Helmut Holtzhauer also represents the party line so far as he sees
Faust as testimony to the transition from feudalistic to capitalistic times and
finds in it extensive criticism of reactionaries (1963), the late president of
the Goethe Society stands above doctrinaire projection of Marxist notions
into it: "For Goethe the social consciousness of which we are speaking was
by no means related to antagonistic classes in the same clear and unambiguous way as Marx later demonstrated. He found himself confronted with
patterns in thought and behavior which appeared to point to certain inborn
dispositions which determine thoughts and actions in individuals" (1970, 11
ff.). Holtzhauer does not actually espouse Goethe's views on this and other
issues, but he does permit Goethe to hold views which do not dovetail
precisely with Marxist dogma and that is intellectual honesty. All in all,
Holtzhauer's is a beautiful essay, bittersweet in retrospect. "Faust and his

world as Goethe brought them on the stage were for him a metaphor, a metaphor for the evanescence of all life and of all conditions. Emergence and passing away constituted for Goethe the impressive cycle in material and in human systems. He is aware of the inadequacy of these systems, as well as of his own poetic ones, in which he sought to capture them" (27 ff.).

With only a few exceptions of this sort, Marxist work piously accepts outmoded notions including an untenable view of the history of science and a consequent timid distrust of each individual's own interpretive power. This trait is of course by no means limited to the East; I could cite many instances in which the jargon and quasi-religious pathos of an older generation of West Germans has been sorrowfully renewed. I will mention only Georg Gustav Wieszner as the most egregious vindication of Hans Schwerte's proposal (p. 334) for a "lengthy quarantine" to contain and eradicate the term "Faustian." However, the main stream of *Faust* criticism outside of East Germany has turned toward treatment of the art work as a formal structure against the background of world literature, while suspending notions of some basic idea or of a philosophical or moral message.

INTERPRETATIONS OF *Faust*—FORM

Harold Jantz may eventually be recognized as most influential in this regard. He asks with perhaps understandable petulance (1968) that all external considerations, like philosophical notions, compositional history, ideas about the "Faustian" be eschewed in favor of "a careful scrutiny of the [entire] work from its own point of view" (p. 363). Like any other artistic composition, *Faust* is characterized by thematic continuity, by parallels and contrasts among its parts. Finding "the great themes that run through the whole of *Faust*" (p. 367) already in its "Dedication," Jantz offers a sample of his "configurational" approach as a foretaste of a promised longer work, *The Form of Faust*. Recognition of *Faust's* artistic unity in terms of a complex interrelationship of its parts became widely popular in the 1960's (Peter Salm [1966], Alan Cottrell [1968 and 1972], Shalom Weyl), and in Germany the influence of Wilhelm Emrich's notions on symbolism was still apparent (Andrew Jaszi, Werner Keller, Ernst Loeb, Wilfried Malsch, Elke Schümann-Heinke).

Goethe encouraged his critics to give free rein to their own associative imagination: "There it is now—however it may have turned out. And if it still contains plenty of problems, by no means offering every answer, still it will please the reader who knows how to follow a look, a gesture, a gentle hint. He will even find more than I was able to offer" (to Sulpiz Boiserée, 8 September 1831). It seems only appropriate that this challenge, so much in the language of the New Criticism, was taken up with greatest alacrity by the Anglo-American tradition. L. A. Willoughby perceived in *Faust* morphological visions developed in Goethe's biological writings, and R. M. Browning applied Goethe's interpretation of systolic and diastolic rhythms to the so-called *Urfaust* in order to argue its artistic development. Eudo C. Mason extended the same sort of perception to the entire *Faust I* at about the time when Rolf Christian Zimmermann's exposition of the hermetic tradition provided unexpected external support. Here the symbolism of contraction and expansion seems central to a complex of cosmic associations.

Paul Requadt's scene-by-scene interpretation of *Faust I* (like Mason, he heeds only Act V in *Faust II*) is predicated on just such an oscillation between expansion and concentration motifs (1972). He traces out an intricate network with much the same stunning effect as that achieved by Wilhelm Emrich for *Faust II* twenty years earlier. Associations within the work (e.g., the leitmotif of "letter and spirit" as related to concentration and expansion) and between *Faust* and other works (e.g., the "expansive" excursion in "Before the City Gates" as analogous to Willhelm's recollection of a boyhood outing in the *Wanderjahre*) are admittedly Requadt's own associations. They would never have satisfied analytic, positivist critics who were concerned with the author's intention as it vacillated over many years and who were therefore able to find unity only in some philosophical idea behind the poem. Requadt's is a vision of *Faust I* developing like a living and moving embryo by systole and diastole in a rich ambience of analogy with itself, world literature and Goethe's other studies. Goethe explicitly asked for imaginative participation from his reader, even demanded it with such scenes as "Walpurgis Night Dream." Requadt shows how this particular chunk of 18th-century reality is prefigured in earlier scenes and how its themes are related to larger leitmotifs. Echoing Jantz, he vows "renunciation of any presumptively pivotal 'idea' in *Faust*, be it moral, philosophical or political, as well as distrust of any harmonious solution" (p. 354). Yet, with Peter Michelsen, he sees Faust's blindness as the center of *Faust II*. It symbolizes Faust's most fundamental, final mistake, "because the fate of a human community depends on him" (p. 376). The final monologue constitutes a return from error, and Requadt chastizes Wilhelm Böhm for not taking this so-called Freedom Vision seriously and not recognizing that "Goethean erring is always directed toward truth" (p. 382). A truly *eingeteufelter* New Critic will no doubt ask Requadt: *Warum machst du Gemeinschaft mit uns, wenn du sie nicht durchführen kannst?*

Of course, we are observing the New Criticism being applied to *Faust* at a time when it is not new at all; hence other approaches may prove more interesting, even when they are less successful. Wolfgang Streicher seeks to show the dramatic unity of *Faust* by means of principles derived from the Goethe-Schiller correspondence and from Emil Staiger's venerable work of the 1930's—and Staiger is the most recent writer appearing in his bibliography. Peter Salm's argument (1971) for morphological unity also offers little new.

Inspired by Katharine Mommsen's source studies, the Anglicist Wilhelm Kleinschmidt von Lengefeld prefers to accept the whole *Faust* as a very loosely organized kind of *Arabian Nights* agglomerate in which the plot is not so important as the kaleidoscopic surroundings and adventures. We should take pleasure in Goethe's inconsequentiality, repetitions, omissions and skipping about. No scene need be interpreted as contributing to development. The "Walpurgis Night" is in its own right an episode in Faust's journey with Mephisto, secondarily perhaps a kind of Satanic companion piece to the Gretchen episode. To relate the "Classical Walpurgis Night" to Helen is "an awkward attempt to produce a plot line" (p. 114). Faust is not a developing hero; he gains nothing from his adventures. The work is essentially epic, perhaps a kind of closet drama.

In an essay marked by its British upper-class hilarity and couched in the language of an ingroup (she begs us to cease sending her letters— p. 163), Elizabeth M. Wilkinson (1971-72) advances the eminently sensible arguments that the competent critic and teacher must be able to perceive works from various vantage points in time and civilization. It is well known how Goethe by his last years had come to recognize that literary works are not islands unto themselves, but continue to exist from one age to the next in posterity's understanding. Hermann Schmitz even felt that Goethe's mode of writing was conditioned by this recognition in his old age (certainly it does constitute one of the most touching themes in the letters from his last years). We have seen how Goethe withheld *Faust II* until after his death, bitterly lashing out at "the times" in a paragraph so harsh that editors of his correspondence suppressed it for many years. At last an era seems to have arrived whose relativistic posture toward issues of principle and whose preoccupation with the more playful and aesthetic potentials of art permit the kind of detachment which might have pleased Goethe.

There can be little doubt that the desperate stodginess of the Germans is mainly responsible for the world's notion that *Faust* is a heavy work in and concerning pathos of the intellect. When one does admit to comical elements, this may occur in the shallowest and most humorless sense—Walter Müller-Seidel (1969) mistakes the Baccalaureus' ridiculous pomp for a quip by urbane Mephistopheles (pp. 98 ff.). Should an author of the 1950s address himself to irony in a chapter set aside for that purpose, as does Erich

Franz, the approach is deeply serious. Franz actually regards irony as a Goethean or Faustian error. *Faust* is said to take us "through complete savoring of error to the truth . . . through the highest degree of ironic play to final seriousness" (146 ff.). Hermann Schmitz is therefore offering a real breakthrough with his acceptance of irony as an ingrained quality in the ancient Goethe's intellect, reality arising for Goethe from a perception of opposites, and ambiguity quite essential for its grasp—not a failing to be overcome. Peter Salm (1966) describes the expansion and intensification of irony as the composition of *Faust* proceeded. At last Ulrich K. Goldsmith, in an essay ostensibly directed at the "general reader," becomes harbinger of a new approach to *Faust* by stressing its deep ambiguity on fundamental issues.

All in the same year (1970) Hans Egon Hass evaluates Goethe's irony positively; Herman Meyer protests eloquently and with profuse documentation that those *Faust* interpretations which demand yes-no answers really miss the whole point and are *Spielverderber*—"spoil sports"; and Harold Jantz offers a lovely illustration by exploring the possibility long entertained by Goethe that Mephistopheles just might in the end be saved. Obviously, irony was in the air of the 1960s.

In an afterword Meyer tells how he met Ehrhard Bahr in California in 1968 just while the younger man was writing his dissertation with the same title as Meyer's own essay (an especially interesting anecdote to me, who was at exactly the same time finishing the MS for this book and fondly imagining that my emphasis on irony was terrifically original—incidentally, also a striking sidelight on relative promptness of publishing here and in Europe). Bahr is dealing with irony in various works by the ancient Goethe, *Faust II* among others. It is his first chapter, where discussion is held on a general level departing from Thomas Mann and Hermann Schmitz, which makes a brilliant presentation of the view that "any question of the work which asks for an unambiguous answer is in Goethe's view simply formulated wrong." Bahr may very well have produced the central work of *Faust* criticism in our decade by recognizing irony as Goethe's characteristic quality and relating it to many of his other attributes as they affect the composition of *Faust*, e.g., his sly secretiveness.

The most able work of the decade has been by scholars addressing themselves to large interests, either like Goldsmith, Dieckmann, and Wilkinson because they have students in mind, or like Andreas Wachsmuth, Paul Böckmann, and Helmut Rehder (1970) who, at the pinnacle of their careers, wish to reach beyond a professional readership. Wachsmuth's perception of *Faust* as Promethean self-assertion against the destructive forces of nature and time represents an older tradition distilled and purified of its questionable implications. Böckmann's essay (originally a 1961 lecture and published for the first time in Dutch, in 1963) is actually on *Faust II*, where the imaginative participation of the reader is supremely important. We are not dealing so much with plot as with a symbolic context in which the associative power must be furnished. For Goethe the concept "symbol" was related to his notion of the *Urphänomen:* a challenge to the imagination, which must surround a central idea with an entire cycle of related images—be they real phenomena or only potentialities. Goethe liked to call this activity *Supplieren,* and Böckmann finds it kin to his concept of mutual mirroring in life and art. Helen and Euphorion are prime examples of figures which demand that the reader produce and unfold extensive associative contexts. *Faust* brings a "cyclic unity of various sectors of life" (p. 197) which it is up to the reader to perceive and interrelate symbolically.

Rehder's is a compact and graceful comprehensive study, twenty pages neatly divided into seven sections which treat specific aspects. The fundamental source of *Faust* is the human drive toward a life of the spirit; in complex cultural, social and historical contexts this drive impinges on the sphere of science as on the sphere of faith. The basic themes are love and knowledge; their endless implications organize Faust's parts as intimately as members in a body. Rehder surveys the varied language, places the dramatic characters in context with contemporary German literature. The metaphorical universe of *Faust* is skillfully related to a larger universe. "Making manifest the two highest principles of existence and contemplation—light and spirit, themselves without form but productive of form—became the main goal of Goethe's life, hence his *Theory of Color* and *Faust* could appear to the aging poet as his most important projects" (p. 164).

These general essays are just about the only ones from our decade that can be recommended for student reading. Lieselotte Dieckmann's slender book has the added advantage of being in English. Hers is a traditional, even somewhat prim (Faust is a "coarse, unscrupulous" "seducer" whose vows of love are "lies"—pp. 52 f.) reading, but remarkably compact, comprehensive, and well informed. Elizabeth Wilkinson's merits (1971) may recommend her more to the teacher: 1) recognition of the student as the indispensable reference point for sound criticism; 2) acceptance of the relativism of all literary commentary, and emphasis on the role played by chance in molding our attitudes; 3) a consequent eagerness to experiment with various models of literary interpretation; 4) emphasis on the theological background of Goethe's work—a minor issue, perhaps, if one takes the long view, but an issue which takes on major importance against the deprived background of our era.

These superb overviews of *Faust* appear modest indeed if compared with the imposing volumes which earlier generations produced. Characteristic of the late 1960s and early 1970s is the absence of the "big book," but it would probably be wrong to infer a decline in the importance of *Faust*. As I earlier urged, German criticism has been only remotely related to the sources. We probably can in the compactness of these publications recognize a decline in the pomp and pathos being permitted the professoriat—and this, in turn, may be in line with a closer return to the text itself. It is also clear that the shorter essay is appropriate to the kind of criticism favored by our time.

INTERPRETATIONS OF INDIVIDUAL SCENES AND FIGURES

Harold Jantz himself exemplified and coined the term "configurational approach" for modern preoccupation with the motif and its symbolic outreach, in line with Goethe's admonition to perceive the parts of an organism as reflected in one another. Other major practitioners of this method are Requadt and Keller. While the result is a programmatic confirmation of artistic unity in the work (projected from the eye of the beholder) the method itself is based on scrutiny of the individual component, usually in a short, well organized essay. Given this tenor of current criticism, it is natural that those scenes and figures have attracted most attention which have in the past appeared most neglected, perhaps because they seemed least essential to the whole work—the preludes, "Walpurgis Night Dream," Act IV. Ernst Grumach and later Joachim Müller (1964) call attention to the prologues as crucial to the whole 1797 *Faust* conception. Alwin Binder's monograph is a tedious treatise which focuses on the Poet and poetological considerations of "Prologue in the Theater." The rather uninspired question raised by Oskar Seidlin as to whether it was really intended as a prelude to *Faust* is answered to the effect that Goethe was in writing it mainly concerned with problems of *Faust II*. Douglas Bub (1969) more successfully—and more succinctly—links this prelude with "Dedication," calls both of them together the "true prologue to *Faust*" (p. 792), and underlines the important themes joining them to the rest of the work. N. Banerjee synthesizes all three preludes in much the same way, e.g., the "Dedication" is not mere spontaneous lyric, but thematically intergrated with the whole drama. The "Prologue in the Theater" renders the whole work "poetry about Poetry." The "Prologue in Heaven" foreshadows plot, philosophy and motifs to come. This work may serve as typical for other treatments of individual scenes by Blume, Bub (1968, 1974), Dietze (1969), Fuchs (1966, 1970), Hippe, Levedahl, Maché, Steffensen, Stelzmann, and Runge.

The shocking remark by Günther Anders, "Faust is dead" (*Der Jahresring*, 1955-6, pp. 86 ff.) reflected the widespread disillusionment among

Germans which was bound to follow upon their earlier manic elevation of the figure. Our time now characteristically pays more attention to other figures in the work than to the protagonist. Mephistopheles has been of perennial interest, but at last we have a book, by Günther Mahal, which follows him "through the ages," before, after, and beside Goethe in a comprehensive survey of devil literature, sacred and profane. In his second section, with about 50 pages out of over 500, Mahal treats *Faust's* "most Christian devil," arguing that the "canonical *Faust* interpretation" (p. 332) has fostered an unjustifiably negative Mephisto image to match its exaggeratedly positive depiction of Faust himself. Furthermore, the drama's thematic structure is so keyed on the Mephistopheles figure that proper interpretation of the work forbids such traditional eclipsing of him. As is so often the case with important insights, this one was anticipated somewhat by Albert Fuchs (1965), Christian Gellinek, and Charles M. Barrack, whose brief articles did not reach Mahal before publication.

Hans Mayer courageously tries to rehabilitate Famulus Wagner by comparing his relatively harmless nature with Faust's dangerous drives (after the line argued by Erich Heller). In the sense of C. P. Snow's two cultures, he argues that Wagner is a humane scientist in the tradition of Giambattista Vico, so that especially our own science-endangered epoch should think twice before it finds him (as Goethe and Faust admittedly do) merely laughable. We have seen how the Marxist critic is prone to relate *Faust* figures to Goethe's or to our own world, and it may be indicative now of Mayer's own career that he continues this tradition not in the party-line optimism but in New World skepticism.

Wilhelm Nauhaus and Kenneth Weisinger are more typical of the current trend, which no longer wishes to look outside the realm of art for aids to interpretation. Nauhaus departs from the image of the rainbow in Act I to pursue it through Goethe's opus aside from *Faust* much as Joachim Müller (1966) does with the cloud formation.

Kenneth Weisinger's perceptive study of the triad Anaxagoras, Thales, Homunculus, on the other hand, shows that the traditional drawing on Goethe's assessment of geological research by the Vulcanists and the Neptunists does not really clarify, but rather obscures structural lines. Following the example of Rehder (1963), he recognizes the relationship of the two teachers, mythogogue and rationalist, as analogous to that of God and Mephistopheles to Faust, and calls it "one of the recurring structural configurations." Other individual figures are treated by Bietak, Fuchs (1961–62), Peterich, Stock, Volkmar, and Wertheim.

Integrationist criticism has given major attention to Act IV. Paul Requadt (1964) perceives the Emperor as an important figure in his own right with a well-rounded personality which undergoes a significant development—one parallel to Faust's. The Emperor episode, with its own plot, content, and image world is analogous to the Helen episode and, like it, intricately related to the whole work. Wolfgang Wittkowski (1967–8) builds on Requadt by seeking to stress the relative importance of Act IV. In Act V, Faust undertakes grand societal goals, while in Act IV it is the Emperor who carefully builds his own political world out of human elements. Fritz Paul shows how the nature symbolism of Act IV conveys Faust's perception of senseless repetition in nature. Mountain heights are symbolic for the spiritual rejuvenation which Faust experiences at the pinnacle of life.

A brilliant article by Leonard Forster (1969–70) casts the arrival of Helen at Faust's castle in a new light and undermines (subsequently published!) interpretations of Lynceus. He shows that Helen's reception included a carefully rehearsed court masque after the mode of the renaissance. Lynceus' "failure" thus becomes a happy play within a play of the sort often witnessed and staged in courtly society (including Weimar).

Konrad Burdach's study of Care was pivotal in bringing about a better balanced view of Faust's entire career, and for a few decades thereafter Care remained one of the figures most frequently studied, especially by writers concerned with an existentialist interpretation. Wolfgang Wittkowski (1967–8), while not entirely free of that tradition, is more interested in integrating the figure structurally. Care is not artistically separable from Guilt, a pair who are active throughout the whole work. The Evil Spirit besetting Gretchen in the Cathedral, Phorkyas confronting Helen with her past deeds, and the Bishop making demands of the Emperor are all prefigurations of Care and her companions.

LITERARY (AND OTHER) ALLUSIONS

Criticism which pursues detailed thematic relationships exemplifies only half of what Jantz calls the configurational approach. Also typical of our era is expansive reconnoitering through world literature, ancient and modern, to capture the full richness of Goethe's allusions. Horst Rüdiger, having already displayed (1963) with *The Golden Ass* some of the "numerous subterranean rivulets which connect the flood of classical literature with our own poetry" (p. 82), goes ahead to show how much of world literature invests the figure of Helen (*JDSD*, 1964). In Act III he singles out six important strands: Greek tragedy, Minnesang and Persian love poetry (Lynceus), the European pastorale (*Arcadia*), the Italian-German opera (*Euphorion*), and modern English poetry (tribute to Byron). Rüdiger (1966) explicitly regards "creative reception" as that intimate joining of borrowing and originality which distinguishes great poetry from the mere clever idea (386), a contention which he also illustrates with Goethe's use of "Arcadia" in poetic tradition (*Die Bühnengenossenschaft*, 1964).

In the 19th century there remained a lot of unexplored, purely factual information about sources and composition of important literary works. Its exantlation was fascinating and often increases appreciation of the works themselves. Need for such basic scholarship naturally declined with its very advance, but scholars have enjoyed doing it and profited from returns to it. Steffen Steffensen is even able to delineate more sharply the complementarity between the harmonious, pietistic realm symbolized by the sign of the macrocosm and the more dynamic, pagan realm of the Earth Spirit. Zimmermann later develops this complex of sources more fully. In our decade, in addition to the authors already mentioned, Aristophanes, Petrarch, Shakespeare, Schiller, Wolfram, and others have been related to *Faust*. Nevertheless, Katharine Mommsen states that source studies have become unfashionable and even scorned. She wished to endow them with unprecedented value: "I shall investigate the insight they provide into the meaning of the work, the task being to perceive their *spiritual* significance" (p. vii). In 1960, with *Goethe und 1001 Nacht*, she displayed Goethe's acquaintance with the *Arabian Nights* and showed their importance for Goethe's techniques in *Faust II*. The most important new interpretation now drawn from her expansion on the same subject is the perception of the roles of Helen and Homunculus. Homunculus does not lead up to Helen, but rather symbolizes the search for life, while Helen is the symbol for beauty in art. Especially incisive is Mommsen's connection of Helen with Mephistopheles, whom she sees in the role of creative artist, conjuring up the Helen Act.

Heinrich Dörrie touches only lightly on Galatea as she appears in Goethe's work (pp. 73–76), but his book on the ancient and modern background of this figure is an important addition to *Faust* studies. In his beautiful treatment of the Mothers Myth, Harold Jantz carries this same comparatist approach into the "poetic process which takes place on a largely subconscious level" (p. 25). It is a fascinating attempt to come to terms with creativity, and as such an extremely important contribution to literary criticism, of which German studies in America can be proud. In singling out ancient and renaissance prefigurations of the Mothers Myth as they may have contributed to its growth in Goethe's developing consciousness, Jantz is not merely pursuing source studies, but criticism with an essentially psychological bent. He states clearly enough (p. 83) that "the final mystery will not be laid bare," but he so impresses us with the importance of the sources which he has uncovered and he makes such strong claims for the significance of the Mothers Myth that his major thrust may be missed by some readers. Because of Goethe's susceptibility to visual impressions, Jantz' most stunning revelation may be the importance of a Hellenistic bas relief for the Mothers concept, *The Apotheosis of Homer*, which Goethe had seen in Rome and also received in plaster cast in 1827. Hans Ost and Gaspard Pinette (1972) have also pointed up the value of true images for the creative process in Goethe, Ost by showing how the language of Act III reflects Helen iconography, Pinette by drawing our attention to the Aurora motif, especially in Tiepolo's paintings.

HISTORY OF COMPOSITION

Alongside these studies of relationships within the realm of art there continues, of course, the old quest for specific individuals who may be reflected in *Faust*, the most conspicuous being perhaps Merck, Madame de Staël, Fr. Schlegel, Klinger, and Schleiermacher. Such issues are at best paraliterary, but our decade was at least graced by one parody so sharp that I want to quote from it. After demonstrating that Erasmus Senkenberg (1717–95) served as model for Faust and for Mephisto on the basis of incredibly tenuous parallels between *Faust* and protocols of Senkenberg's legal entanglements: "If we had not already cited the drinking and duelling scenes as sources for *Faust*, it would be all too bold to discover a source for *Faust* in these papers as well. However, since it has become obvious how freely Goethe handled the materials . . . to accommodate them to his ideas, it is no doubt permissible to pinpoint the following borrowings as well" (p. 153). Engelsing is clearly arguing that positivism has outlived its usefulness. That this is not the case can be seen from the excellent progress made in illuminating the history of composition.

Heinz Bluhm, whose exquisitely close scrutiny of Luther's Bible translation has proved so rewarding, performed a similar service with the first version of Faust's final monologue, demonstrating that once we get to a true reading of the manuscript the speech appears to have shown good continuity from its conception. Bernt von Heiseler compares the Dungeon Scene with its rendition in the Göchhausen manuscript to show how Goethe managed to bring out nuance, experience, and humanity in revision.

In executing the most careful analysis to date of the manuscript evidence for the "Walpurgis Night" (1965), Siegfried Scheibe also illuminates other aspects of the history of composition of *Faust I*, showing, for example, that its publication in 1806 was preceded by a flurry of activity after the material had lain incomplete for several years. Scheibe's main strength is that he never loses sight of Goethe's work habits, about which he teaches us a great deal as he keeps reminding us of them. In attempting to settle the dispute as to the exact manuscript form of the early *Faust* (1967), Scheibe shows that Goethe's habits must have remained substantially the same from his youth into advanced years. The work on *Poetry and Truth*, for example, proceeded both in the form of extensive, coherent manuscript and provisionally unincorporated jottings. One of Scheibe's major contributions is clarification of the confusion created by Erich Schmidt when he called the Göchhausen manuscript the *Urfaust*. Scheibe recommends (1970) that we abjure the term entirely. If it is *Faust* in some undetermined stage prior to its fragmentary first publication we are talking about, simply "the early *Faust*" will do. If, on the other hand, we wish to speak of those scenes which chance captured for us in Louise von Göchhausen's copy, then Scheibe would have us call it that. Here Scheibe's thinking may owe something to Wolfgang Binder's perception of the *Faust* composition as ongoing flux which we need to distinguish in our minds from those occasional precipitates which happen to have been preserved.

Ernst Grumach had called renewed attention to the *Faust* plan of 1797, of which limited but important manuscript traces remain. Binder, in a reversion to older, ideological interpretation, attempts to construct a vision of that 1797 conception of the art work as it might have existed at the "classical" stage. "The symbolism in Faust, and his path, demand a totality of the series; similarly structured developments must be joined to him if at the end the 'idea' itself is to be conveyed" (p. 88). Binder bases his speculation on the enigmatic polarities indicated by so-called Paralipomenon 1, which seems to represent a Goethean attempt to capture the quintessence of the *Faust* concept in 1800. Not only does Binder feel that "entire portions of *Faust II*" (p. 86) are prefigured in that 98-word sketch, but he argues that the unity of the entire work can be inferred from this particular stage.

We have Goethe's word for it that he arranged the *Faust* materials in large masses in 1797, which he apparently numbered (the manuscript numbers 16, 17, 20, 22, 24, 27, 28, 30 survive). Horst Schulze makes a brave effort to reconstruct this 1797 version, and he did at least succeed in provoking another valuable contribution by Siegfried Scheibe on Goethe's work habits (1972). Scheibe reminds us that the 1797 plan was still for a one-part *Faust*, the idea of a second part arising perhaps around 1800. The numbers preserved on certain paralipomena do not refer to scenes, but to groupings extending over the entire *Faust* and each perhaps eventually becoming, or already containing, several scenes. These sections were partly already written, partly just planned, the purpose of the 1797 sketches being to draw completed and projected work together. Compared to that ground plan, what was actually executed for *Faust I* was just a fragment, no more than that portion which Goethe felt he could finish fairly quickly. The postponed portions were, of course, to take on a radically different character before they were incorporated into the work many years later. Scheibe emphatically despairs of reconstructing the 1797 concept from the meager materials we have, but his work gives numerous hints which, if followed up, do promise better understanding, e.g., the recognition that, since the 1797 plan must have been given up around 1800, manuscript materials *without* numbers integrating them into it are probably post 1800.

CONCLUSION

Can we in conclusion make any generalizations about recent *Faust* scholarship which would at the same time permit conjecture about the future? Paul Requadt is impressed by the shift of the center of gravity, as it were, toward Anglo-American critics and, even among the Germans, toward approaches originating in America and England. This shift has meant extreme refinement in methodology at the sacrifice of rationale based in contemporary needs and interests. By contrast, Marxist critics continue to study *Faust* as a repository of values sanctioned by their society. This places them at an apparent moral advantage over their Western colleagues in that they have a clear justification for what they are doing. They are writing for a public, and they have specific societal ends in view beyond personal aesthetic experience.

The exquisitely sensitive and highly sophisticated work of Western critics may contrast startlingly with the crude, politically motivated work of their Marxist brothers, but it remains self-contained—critics read only each other and by only each other are read. The irony of the situation in the West is of course that the new and important insights achieved there do indeed speak to major problems being encountered in the other sectors of society. What literary criticism has to say about the nature of our perceptions, the potentials of human imagination and craftmanship, the need and possibility of ethical restraints, etc., is of great practical importance in the most diverse areas, to the physicist, the engineer, the social scientist, the biologist. They have long since discovered *Faust;* it is unlikely, however, that they can discover *Faust* criticism before the *Faust* critic discovers them. My prediction would be that *Faust* scholarship will discover these significant reaches of the intellect to a constantly greater degree, and that such discovery will distinguish future work much as concentration on the text itself has distinguished the past decade.

Böckmann, Dieckmann, Goldsmith, Rehder and Wilkinson already seem tacitly to be conceding that *Faust* research has now passed through an important systolic phase in which it stored up a great potential wealth but did not manage to seek out or develop channels for distributing it. A new phase of diastole already finds them and will no doubt find others turning proven energies outward. We shall have to explore new realms of the intellect until we know them and their problems well enough to create needed linkages. This will not mean deemphasis or debasement of our own field, or dilletantism in others. We have quite simply reached a point, like biology at the middle of our century, where we can go no further without broadening our base. One of the major gains in recent *Faust* criticism has already been full appreciation of the intricate interdependence and mutual mirroring of all parts in a system, so that the one part is not trivialized, but rather takes on full dimensionality in the mind able to overview the larger context.

INDEX

TO FAUST TEXT

TOPICAL INDEX